# favourite
# hot & spicy

over 100 recipes to enjoy

First published in 2010

LOVE FOOD is an imprint of Parragon Books Ltd

Parragon

Queen Street House

4 Queen Street

Bath BA1 1HE, UK

ISBN: 978-1-4075-4763-3

Printed in China

Cover design by Andrew Easton at Ummagumma
Internal design by the Bridgewater Book Company Ltd
Recipes by Mridula Baljekar, Elisabeth Luard, Corinne Trang and Judy Williams
Photography by Clive Bozzard-Hill, Laurie Evans and Clive Streeter
Food styling by Valerie Barrett, Angela Drake, Emma Jane Frost and Carol Tennant

Notes for the Reader

This book uses both metric and imperial measurements. Follow the same units of measurement throughout; do not mix metric and imperial. All spoon measurements are level: teaspoons are assumed to be 5 ml, and tablespoons are assumed to be 15 ml. Unless otherwise stated, milk is assumed to be full fat, eggs and individual vegetables are medium, and pepper is freshly ground black pepper.

The times given are an approximate guide only. Preparation times differ according to the techniques used by different people and the cooking times may also vary from those given. Optional ingredients, variations or serving suggestions have not been included in the calculations.

Recipes using raw or very lightly cooked eggs should be avoided by infants, the elderly, pregnant women, convalescents and anyone suffering from an illness. Pregnant and breastfeeding women are advised to avoid eating peanuts and peanut products. Sufferers from nut allergies should be aware that some of the ready-made ingredients used in the recipes in this book may contain nuts. Always check the packaging before use.

Vegetarians should be aware that some of the ready-made ingredients used in the recipes in this book may contain animal products. Always check the packaging before use.

Take great care when preparing chillies, as the juice is very painful if transferred to eyes or other sensitive parts of the body. Wash your hands thoroughly after preparation. To avoid direct contact, use a fork to hold the chillies still while slicing and deseeding with a sharp knife, or wear a new pair of rubber gloves.

# Contents

# Vietnamese 172

# Introduction

The great era of worldwide exploration in the fifteenth and sixteenth centuries was fuelled in part by the European search for spices from the East to preserve the meat of livestock slaughtered before winter fodder ran out. The inadvertent 'discovery' of the Americas may have been a gigantic leap in world history, but by introducing the chilli to Asia, then the Middle East, Africa and Europe, Spanish and Portuguese explorers performed an invaluable service to food lovers everywhere. During the seventeenth century, spices became so precious and expensive that they were used instead of hard currency to pay taxes and when purchasing land. Even today, saffron remains very costly because its production is so labour-intensive, but fortunately most spices are readily available and easily affordable.

It is impossible to imagine food without spices nowadays, whether sweet and fragrant such as coriander and cinnamon, warming and aromatic such as cumin and ginger, or fiery and flavoursome such as chillies and cayenne pepper. They are what add vitality, piquancy, originality and excitement to both savoury and sweet dishes. Of course, there is far more to preparing delicious well-seasoned food than simply adding a spoonful or two of ground spice or a chopped fresh chilli. While cooking with spices is universal, in some countries it has become a real art.

This book celebrates and explores four such cuisines – those of India, Thailand, Vietnam and Latin America – with an impressive collection of authentic recipes from each region, capturing their unique flavour and character. Whether your taste is for a creamy Indian korma, a palate-tingling Thai green curry, fragrant kebabs from Vietnam, or tangy Mexican marinated fish, you are sure to find the perfect dish and will almost certainly be inspired to take an edible global voyage to try other, less familiar spicy specialities.

Each section of the book features four chapters of classic recipes for all occasions. They all include fabulous spicy main courses, but the individual chapters vary to reflect the different culinary traditions of the region. This makes it easy to prepare a complete meal that is authentic in every way and to select individual favourites, whether appetizers, accompaniments, snacks, salads or desserts.

## Storing and using spices

Whether made from seeds, berries, stems, buds, bark, pods or roots, dried spices lose their aroma, colour and pungency quite rapidly, so it is best to buy them in small quantities unless you use them very frequently. Whole spices last longer and are easier to toast in a dry frying pan than ground ones, which may scorch. Most whole spices can be easily ground using a mortar with a pestle or in a spice mill. However, there are a few spices, such as cinnamon, that are virtually impossible to grind at home.

Store both whole and ground spices in airtight glass containers in a cool, dark place. While jars of spices look very attractive in a rack on the kitchen wall, heat and light will speed up the loss of the volatile essential oils that give them their flavour and fragrance. If you must have them on display, use tinted glass jars. As a general rule, ground spices will not keep successfully for more than about six months.

If you are using unfamiliar spices, it is often sensible to add half the quantity suggested in the recipe to begin with, then taste the dish while it is cooking and add more if you like. Whatever you do, do not measure ground spices into a teaspoon or tablespoon directly over the pan – if you overfill the spoon and the spice tips into the pan, you will probably ruin whatever you are cooking. If you are using whole spices in a recipe, check the serving instructions as some, such as cinnamon sticks, lemon grass stalks and star anise, should be removed at the end of cooking, as they taste very unpleasant if you mistakenly put them into your mouth.

Some spices are used while they are still fresh and these will usually taste rather different from the dried versions. In the case of fresh and ground ginger, this is particularly noticeable and they are rarely interchangeable. Ginger and the closely related South East Asian spice galangal are both roots. When buying, look for plump specimens that are as smooth as possible. Peel thinly with a vegetable peeler or sharp paring knife and chop, slice or grate according to the recipe. Lemon grass is widely used in Thai and Vietnamese cooking. Only the bulbous base and the first 4–5 cm/$1\frac{1}{2}$–2 inches of the stem are used. It may be thinly sliced or chopped or lightly crushed and used whole (remove before serving).

Fresh chillies are used extensively in all four regions. It is always difficult to estimate the heat of chillies as one chilli may be mild while another from the same plant is fiery hot. As a general rule, dark green chillies are hotter than pale green, while red chillies are usually milder than both. Small pointed chillies tend to be much hotter than short blunt ones, although the squashed-up round Scotch bonnet chillies are so blisteringly hot they can bring tears to the eyes. Although there are hundreds of varieties, only a limited number are found in most shops and markets, so it is quite difficult to know what you are buying. The heat of chillies is concentrated in the membranes – not in the seeds, as many people think. However, deseeding chillies also removes the membranes and makes them milder. It is a matter of personal choice whether you do this. Do be careful when handling chillies and avoid touching your eyes or other sensitive parts of your body until you have thoroughly washed your hands in warm soapy water. If you have particularly sensitive skin, wear rubber gloves or use a knife and fork when preparing fresh chillies.

# Indian

Spectacular natural beauty, endearing local customs, ancient cultures and glorious food all conspire to captivate the visitor to India, making it impossible to leave without great reluctance.

The vibrant colours, exciting textures and complex flavours of Indian cuisine, produced by the range of spices used, have made Indian food popular the world over. It is also these spices that lured a host of foreign powers to India, resulting in an exotic cuisine with a venerable history.

# Appetizers

The success of a meal depends to a large extent on how it begins, and you can be sure to tantalize the taste buds with these starters. Kebabs are easy to prepare and ideal for both outdoor and indoor dining, and there are several kinds to choose from here, while crisp, deep-fried *bhajiyas* and freshly baked *samosas* are simply irresistible.

The overall presentation of a starter, even for the simplest dish, is greatly enhanced if colour and texture are used imaginatively. A few snipped fresh chives, finely chopped fresh coriander leaves and red and green chilli rings can all add an inviting touch. Fresh fruits are another way of enhancing the presentation of snacks and starters.

# Creamy chicken tikka

*Murgh tikka malai*

**Serves 4**

700 g/1 lb 9 oz skinless, boneless chicken breasts, cut into 2.5-cm/ 1-inch cubes

2 tbsp lemon juice

1/2 tsp salt, or to taste

125 g/41/2 oz whole milk natural yogurt, strained

3 tbsp double cream

25 g/1 oz mild Cheddar cheese, grated

1 tbsp garlic purée

1 tbsp ginger purée

1/2–1 tsp chilli powder

1/2 tsp ground turmeric

1/2 tsp granulated sugar

1 tbsp gram flour, sifted

1 tsp garam masala

2 tbsp sunflower or olive oil, plus 2 tbsp for brushing

3 tbsp melted butter or olive oil

salad, to garnish

Mint and Spinach Chutney, to serve (see page 69)

There are several versions of this ever-popular dish, and this one is quite special. Grated mild Cheddar cheese and cream are added to the marinade, and the combination of the dairy ingredients has a magical effect in tenderizing the meat.

Put the chicken cubes in a non-reactive bowl and add the lemon juice and salt. Rub well into the meat. Cover and leave to marinate in the refrigerator for 20–30 minutes.

Put the yogurt in a separate non-reactive bowl and beat with a fork until smooth. Add all the remaining ingredients, except the melted butter. Beat well until the ingredients are fully incorporated. Add the chicken and mix thoroughly until fully coated with the marinade. Cover and leave to marinate in the refrigerator for 4–6 hours, or overnight. Return to room temperature before cooking.

Preheat the grill on high for 7–8 minutes. Brush 6 metal skewers generously with the remaining 2 tablespoons of oil and thread on the chicken

cubes. Brush any remaining marinade over the tikkas. Place the prepared skewers in a grill pan and grill about 7.5 cm/3 inches below the heat source for 4–5 minutes. Brush generously with the melted butter and cook for a further 1–2 minutes. Turn over and cook for 3–4 minutes, basting frequently with the remaining melted butter.

Balance the skewers over a large saucepan or frying pan and leave to rest for 5–6 minutes before sliding the tikkas off the skewers with a table knife. Serve garnished with salad and accompanied by the chutney.

# Silky chicken kebabs

## *Reshmi kebab*

These ground chicken breasts have a silky texture and an enticing flavour imparted by a cashew cream mixture and garam masala. The taste is subtle yet assertive, allowing you to appreciate the flavours of the different spices as well as the meat.

**Makes 8**

55 g/2 oz cashew nuts

2 tbsp single cream

1 egg

450 g/1 lb skinless, boneless chicken breasts, roughly chopped

1/2 tsp salt, or to taste

2 tsp garlic purée

2 tsp ginger purée

2 green chillies, roughly chopped (deseeded if you like)

15 g/1/2 oz fresh coriander, including the tender stalks, roughly chopped

1 tsp garam masala

vegetable oil, for brushing

25 g/1 oz butter, melted

**To serve**

Mint and Spinach Chutney, to serve (see page 69)

mixed salad

Put the cashew nuts in a heatproof bowl, cover with boiling water and leave to soak for 20 minutes. Drain and put in a food processor. Add the cream and egg and process the ingredients to a coarse mixture.

Add all the remaining ingredients, except the oil and melted butter, and process until smooth. Transfer to a bowl, cover and chill in the refrigerator for 30 minutes.

Preheat the grill on high for 7–8 minutes. Brush the grill rack and 8 metal skewers lightly with oil. Have a bowl of cold water ready.

Divide the chilled mixture into 8 equal-sized portions. Dip your hands into the bowl of cold water – this will stop the mixture sticking to your fingers when you are moulding it onto the skewers. Carefully mould each portion onto the skewers, patting and stretching it gently into a 15-cm/6-inch sausage shape. Arrange the kebabs on the prepared rack and cook about 15 cm/6 inches below the heat source for 4 minutes. Brush with half the melted butter and cook for a further 1 minute. Turn over and cook for 3 minutes. Baste with the remaining melted butter and cook for a further 2 minutes.

Remove from the heat and leave the kebabs to rest for 5 minutes before sliding them off the skewers with a table knife. Serve with the chutney and a mixed salad.

### Cook's tip

The kebabs can be frozen once cooked, but remove them from the heat before the stage where you baste with melted butter and cook for a further 2 minutes. When required, thaw and place under a preheated high grill, baste with the melted butter and cook for 2 minutes on each side.

# Tandoori chicken

## *Tandoori murgh*

4 chicken pieces, about 225 g/
8 oz each, skinned

juice of 1/2 lemon

1/2 tsp salt, or to taste

85 g/3 oz whole milk natural yogurt,
strained, or Greek-style yogurt

3 tbsp double cream

1 tbsp gram flour

1 tbsp garlic purée

1 tbsp ginger purée

1/2–1 tsp chilli powder

1 tsp ground coriander

1/2 tsp ground cumin

1/2 tsp garam masala

1/2 tsp ground turmeric

2 tbsp vegetable oil, for brushing

3 tbsp melted butter or olive oil

salad, to serve

lemon wedges, to garnish

This dish from the North-west Frontier is made with chicken on the bone, which is marinated with natural yogurt as the tenderizer. The yogurt is spiced with garlic, ginger, chilli and garam masala. You can cook the chicken on a barbecue or the grill.

Make 2–3 small incisions in each chicken piece – this will help the flavours penetrate deeper into the meat. Put the chicken pieces in a large non-reactive bowl. Rub in the lemon juice and salt, cover and leave to marinate in the refrigerator for 20 minutes.

Meanwhile, put the yogurt in a separate non-reactive bowl and add the cream and gram flour. Beat with a fork until well blended and smooth. Add all the remaining ingredients, except the oil and melted butter, and mix until the ingredients are thoroughly incorporated. Pour the mixture over the chicken and rub in well. Cover and leave to marinate in the refrigerator for 4–6 hours, or overnight. Return to room temperature before cooking.

Preheat the grill on high for 10 minutes. Line a grill pan with foil and brush the rack with oil. Using tongs, lift the chicken pieces out of the marinade and put on the prepared rack, reserving the remaining marinade. Cook the chicken about 12.5 cm/5 inches below the heat source for 4 minutes. Turn over and cook for a further 4 minutes. Baste the chicken generously with the reserved marinade and cook for a further 2 minutes on each side.

Brush the chicken with the melted butter and cook about 10 cm/4 inches below the heat source for 5–6 minutes, or until charred in patches. Turn over and baste with the remaining marinade. Cook for a further 5–6 minutes, or until charred as before, tender and the juices run clear when a skewer is inserted into the thickest part of the meat.

Transfer the chicken to a dish and serve with a salad, garnished with lemon wedges.

### Cook's tip
This dish freezes well. Thaw completely before reheating in the centre of a preheated oven at 190°C/375°F/Gas Mark 5 for 20–25 minutes, wrapped in a double thickness of foil.

# Marinated lamb brochettes

## Boti shashlik

Serves 4

700 g/1 lb 9 oz boned leg of lamb,
cut into 2.5-cm/1-inch cubes

2 tbsp light malt vinegar

1/2 tsp salt, or to taste

1 tbsp garlic purée

1 tbsp ginger purée

115 g/4 oz whole milk natural
yogurt, strained, or Greek-style
yogurt

1 tbsp gram flour

1 tsp ground cumin

1 tsp garam masala

1/2–1 tsp chilli powder

1/2 tsp ground turmeric

3 tbsp olive or sunflower oil, plus
1 tbsp for brushing

1/2 red pepper, cut into 2.5-cm/
1-inch pieces

1/2 green pepper, cut into 2.5-cm/
1-inch pieces

8 shallots, halved

55 g/2 oz butter, melted

lemon wedges, to serve

Here, tender cubes of lamb are infused with a spice-laced yogurt marinade, skewered with red peppers and shallots, and grilled. The quality of the meat is of prime importance, and be sure to trim off any excess fat before cutting it into cubes.

Put the meat in a large non-reactive bowl and add the vinegar, salt and garlic and ginger purées. Mix together thoroughly, cover and leave to marinate in the refrigerator for 30 minutes.

Put the yogurt and gram flour in a separate bowl and beat together with a fork until smooth. Add the cumin, garam masala, chilli powder, turmeric and oil and mix together thoroughly. Add the yogurt mixture to the marinated meat, then add the peppers and shallots and stir until all the ingredients are well blended. Cover and leave to marinate in the refrigerator for 2–3 hours, or overnight. Return to room temperature before cooking.

Preheat the grill to high. Line the grill pan with a piece of foil. Brush the rack generously with some of the oil and brush 4 metal skewers with the remaining oil.

Thread the marinated lamb, peppers and shallots alternately onto the prepared skewers. Place the skewers on the prepared rack and cook about 7.5 cm/3 inches below the heat source for 4 minutes. Brush generously with half the melted butter and cook for a further 2 minutes. Turn over and cook for 3–4 minutes. Brush with the remaining butter and cook for a further 2 minutes.

Balance the skewers over a large saucepan or frying pan and leave to rest for 5–6 minutes before sliding the kebabs off the skewers with a table knife. Serve with the lemon wedges.

# Lamb kebabs

## Gosht ke seekh

**Makes 8**

55 g/2 oz cashew nuts

3 tbsp double cream

1 egg

1 tbsp gram flour

2 green chillies, roughly chopped

2 shallots roughly chopped

450 g/1 lb fresh lamb mince

1 tsp salt, or to taste

2 tsp garlic purée

2 tsp ginger purée

1 tsp ground cumin

1 tsp garam masala

1 tbsp chopped fresh mint leaves

2 tbsp chopped fresh
coriander leaves

1/2 red pepper, finely chopped

2 tbsp vegetable oil, for brushing

55 g/2 oz butter, melted

*To serve*

rocket leaves, dressed with a little
olive oil

Mint and Spinach Chutney, to serve
(see page 69)

The Indian word for skewer is *seekh*. Traditionally, these kebabs are moulded onto metal skewers and grilled in the Indian clay oven known as a *tandoor*. However, they lend themselves well to cooking under a gas grill or over a charcoal barbecue.

Put the cashew nuts in a heatproof bowl, cover with boiling water and leave to soak for 20 minutes. Drain and put in a food processor. Add the cream and egg and process the ingredients to a coarse mixture.

Add all the remaining ingredients, except the herbs, red pepper, oil and melted butter, and process until thoroughly mixed. Transfer the mixture to a large bowl. Add the herbs and red pepper and mix well. Cover and chill in the refrigerator for 30–40 minutes.

Preheat the grill on high for 10 minutes. Brush the grill rack and 8 metal skewers lightly with oil. Have a bowl of cold water ready.

Divide the chilled mixture into 8 equal-sized portions. Dip your hands into the bowl of cold water – this will stop the mixture sticking to your fingers when you are moulding it onto the skewers. Carefully mould each portion onto the skewers, patting and stretching it gently into a 15-cm/6-inch sausage shape. Arrange the kebabs on the prepared rack and cook about 15 cm/6 inches below the heat source for 4 minutes. Brush with half the melted butter and cook for a further 1 minute. Turn over and cook for 3 minutes. Baste with the remaining melted butter and cook for a further 2 minutes.

Remove from the heat and leave the kebabs to rest for 5 minutes before sliding them off the skewers with a table knife. Arrange the kebabs on a bed of the dressed rocket leaves. Serve immediately with the Mint and Spinach Chutney.

# Fish tikka

## *Mahi tikka*

**Makes 8**

pinch of saffron threads, pounded

1 tbsp hot milk

85 g/3 oz Greek-style yogurt

1 tbsp garlic purée

1 tbsp ginger purée

1 tsp salt, or to taste

1/2 tsp granulated sugar

juice of 1/2 lemon

1/2–1 tsp chilli powder

1/2 tsp garam masala

1 tsp ground fennel seeds

2 tsp gram flour

750 g/1 lb 10 oz salmon fillets, skinned and cut into 5-cm/ 2-inch cubes

olive oil, for brushing

lemon wedges, to serve

*To garnish*

sliced tomatoes

sliced cucumber

You need a firm-fleshed fish for these delectable tikkas. Salmon has been used here, but monkfish produces an equally delicious result, although the unique characteristics of the two different fish give a distinct variation in flavour.

Soak the pounded saffron in the hot milk for 10 minutes.

Put all the remaining ingredients, except the fish and oil, in a bowl and beat with a fork or a wire whisk until smooth. Stir in the saffron and milk, mix well and add the fish cubes. Using a metal spoon, mix gently, turning the fish around until fully coated with the marinade. Cover and leave to marinate in the refrigerator for 2 hours. Return to room temperature before cooking.

Preheat the grill on high for 10 minutes. Brush the grill rack generously with oil and 8 metal skewers lightly with oil. Line the grill pan with a piece of foil. Thread the fish cubes onto the prepared skewers, leaving a narrow gap between each piece. Arrange on the prepared rack and cook about 10 cm/4 inches below the heat source for 3 minutes. Brush the kebabs with oil and cook for a further 1 minute. Turn over and brush any remaining marinade over the fish. Cook for 3 minutes. Brush the fish with more oil and cook for a further 2 minutes, or until the fish is lightly charred.

Remove from the heat and leave to rest for 5 minutes. Garnish with tomatoes and cucumber, and serve with lemon wedges for squeezing over.

# Spicy onion fritters

## Onion bhajiyas

Serves 4

150 g/5½ oz gram flour

1 tsp salt, or to taste

small pinch of bicarbonate of soda

25 g/1 oz ground rice

1 tsp fennel seeds

1 tsp cumin seeds

2 green chillies, finely chopped
(deseeded if you like)

2 large onions, about 400 g/14 oz,
sliced into half-rings and separated

15 g/½ oz fresh coriander,
including the tender stalks,
finely chopped

200 ml/7 fl oz water

sunflower or olive oil,
for deep-frying

tomato or mango chutney, to serve

These fritters are quick and easy to make, and seriously delicious. Note the spelling of bhajiya, which is the correct version, meaning a deep-fried snack, rather than the commonly used bhaji, which simply means a vegetable side dish.

Sift the gram flour into a large bowl and add the salt, bicarbonate of soda, ground rice and fennel and cumin seeds. Mix together thoroughly, then add the chillies, onions and coriander. Gradually pour in the water and mix until a thick batter is formed and all the other ingredients are thoroughly coated with it.

Heat enough oil for deep-frying in a wok, deep saucepan or deep-fat fryer to 180–190°C/340–350°F, or until a cube of bread browns in 30 seconds. If the oil is not hot enough, the bhajiyas will be soggy. Add as many small amounts (about ½ tablespoon) of the batter as will fit in a single layer, without overcrowding. Reduce the heat slightly and cook the bhajiyas for 8–10 minutes, until golden brown and crisp. Maintaining a steady temperature is important to ensure that the centres of the bhajiyas are cooked, while the outsides turn brown. Remove and drain on kitchen paper. Keep hot in a low oven while you cook the remaining batter.

Serve hot with a tomato or mango chutney.

# Crispy vegetable triangles

## *Vegetable samosas*

Samosas are one of the most popular snacks in India, and the original recipe is vegetarian. Traditionally, a rich pastry is made at home, but filo pastry is used here, which works extremely well and reduces the preparation time considerably.

**Makes 12**

3 tbsp sunflower or olive oil

1/2 tsp black mustard seeds

1 tsp cumin seeds

1 tsp fennel seeds

1 onion, finely chopped

2 green chillies, finely chopped (deseeded if you like)

2 tsp ginger purée

1/2 tsp ground turmeric

1 tsp ground coriander

1 tsp ground cumin

1/2 tsp chilli powder

350 g/12 oz boiled potatoes, cut into bite-sized pieces

125 g/4 1/2 oz frozen peas, thawed

1 tsp salt, or to taste

2 tbsp chopped fresh coriander leaves

12 sheets filo pastry, about 28 x 18 cm/11 x 7 inches

55 g/2 oz butter, melted, plus extra for greasing

chutney, to serve

Heat the oil in a saucepan over a medium heat and add the mustard seeds, followed by the cumin and fennel seeds. Add the onion, chillies and ginger purée and cook, stirring frequently, for 5–6 minutes, until the onion is soft but not brown.

Add the ground spices and cook, stirring, for 1 minute. Add the potatoes, peas and salt and stir until the vegetables are thoroughly coated with the spices. Stir in the coriander and remove from the heat. Leave to cool completely.

Preheat the oven to 180°C/350°F/Gas Mark 4 and line a baking sheet with greased greaseproof paper or baking paper.

Place a sheet of filo pastry on a board and brush well with the melted butter. Keep the remaining pastry sheets covered with a moist cloth or clingfilm. Fold the buttered pastry sheet in half lengthways, brush with some more melted butter and fold lengthways again.

Place about 1 tablespoon of the vegetable filling on the bottom right-hand corner of the pastry sheet and fold over to form a triangle. Continue folding to the top of the sheet, maintaining the triangular shape, and moisten the ends to seal the edges. Transfer to the prepared baking sheet and brush with melted butter. Repeat with the remaining sheets of filo pastry and filling.

Bake the samosas in the preheated oven just below the top rung of the oven for 20 minutes, or until browned. Serve hot with chutney.

# Main Courses

A collection of simplified classic Indian main dishes has been recreated here, including a chicken korma from Delhi enriched with pistachio nuts, the famous slow-cooked lamb dish *rogan josh* from the foothills of the Himalayas and a coconut-based fish curry from Goa.

Choose the leanest possible meat and follow cooking temperatures carefully. In Indian cooking, the skin of chicken is always removed to allow the spices and other flavours to penetrate. Always make sure that fish and shellfish are absolutely fresh when you buy them, and that the period of time between purchasing and cooking is as short as possible. All the dishes can be frozen – thaw in the refrigerator before reheating.

# Kashmiri lamb curry

## *Rogan josh*

**Serves 4**

4 tbsp sunflower or olive oil

1 large onion, roughly chopped

5-cm/2-inch piece fresh ginger, peeled and roughly chopped

5 large garlic cloves, roughly chopped

400 g/14 oz canned tomatoes

3 brown cardamom pods

2 bay leaves

1 tbsp ground coriander

1 tsp ground turmeric

1 tsp chilli powder

700 g/1 lb 9 oz boned leg of lamb, cut into 2.5-cm/1-inch cubes

150 g/5½ oz natural yogurt

2 tsp gram flour

1 tsp salt, or to taste

1 tbsp tomato purée

125 ml/4 fl oz warm water

1 tsp ghee or unsalted butter

1 tsp garam masala

½ tsp ground nutmeg

2 tbsp chopped fresh coriander leaves

naan or plain boiled basmati rice, to serve

This deliciously spiced lamb dish from the Himalayan region is traditionally cooked with a brilliantly coloured variety of chillies. This colour can be replicated by mixing chilli powder with Hungarian paprika and a touch of tomato purée.

Heat 2 tablespoons of the oil in a medium-sized, heavy-based saucepan over a medium heat. Add the onion, ginger and garlic and cook, stirring frequently, for 5 minutes, or until lightly coloured. Remove from the heat and squeeze out as much excess oil as possible from the onion mixture by pressing against the side of the saucepan. Transfer the onion mixture to a blender or food processor with the tomatoes and their juice, blend to a purée and set aside.

Return the saucepan to a low heat and add the remaining oil. Add the cardamom pods and bay leaves and leave to sizzle gently for 20–25 seconds, then add the ground coriander, turmeric and chilli powder. Cook, stirring, for 1 minute, then add the tomato mixture. Increase the heat to medium and continue to cook for 10–12 minutes, until the oil separates from the spice paste, reducing the heat to low towards the last 2–3 minutes.

Add the lamb and increase the heat slightly. Cook, stirring, until the meat changes colour.

Put the yogurt and gram flour in a bowl and beat together with a fork or wire whisk until smooth. Reduce the heat slightly and stir the yogurt mixture, 2 tablespoons at a time, into the meat mixture. Add the salt and tomato purée. Reduce the heat to low, cover and cook for 30 minutes, stirring occasionally.

Add the water and bring it to a slow simmer. Re-cover and cook for a further 20–25 minutes, until the meat is tender.

Melt the ghee in a small saucepan over a low heat, add the garam masala and nutmeg and cook, stirring, for 30 seconds. Pour the spiced butter over the curry and stir in half the chopped fresh coriander. Remove from the heat and serve garnished with the remaining fresh coriander, accompanied by naan or plain boiled basmatic rice.

# Lamb in fragrant spinach sauce

## *Saag gosht*

Serves 4

700 g/1 lb 9oz boned leg of lamb

85 g/3 oz whole milk natural yogurt, strained, or Greek-style yogurt

2 tbsp light malt vinegar

2 tsp gram flour

1 tsp ground turmeric

4 tbsp sunflower or olive oil

5-cm/2-inch piece cinnamon stick, halved

5 cloves

5 green cardamom pods, bruised

2 bay leaves

1 large onion, finely chopped

2 tsp garlic purée

2 tsp ginger purée

2 tsp ground cumin

1/2–1 tsp chilli powder

200 g/7 oz canned tomatoes

175 ml/6 fl oz warm water, plus 4 tbsp

1 tsp salt, or to taste

1 tsp sugar

250 g/9 oz spinach leaves, thawed if frozen, chopped

2 tsp ghee or unsalted butter

1 large garlic clove, finely chopped

1/4 tsp freshly grated nutmeg

1 tsp garam masala

125 ml/4 fl oz single cream

Chilli-coriander Naan (see page 76) or plain boiled basmati rice, to serve

This robust, home-style dish hails from the northern state of the Punjab, where people love good food drenched in home-made butter! *Saag gosht* is traditionally eaten with bread such as naan or paratha, but it tastes equally good with rice.

Trim the excess fat from the meat and cut into 2.5-cm/1-inch cubes. Put the yogurt in a non-reactive bowl and beat with a fork or wire whisk until smooth. Add the vinegar, gram flour and turmeric and beat again until well blended. Add the meat and mix thoroughly, cover and leave to marinate in the refrigerator for 4–5 hours, or overnight. Return to room temperature before cooking.

Heat the oil in a medium-sized, heavy-based saucepan over a low heat. Add the cinnamon, cloves, cardamom pods and bay leaves and cook gently, stirring, for 25–30 seconds, then add the onion. Increase the heat to medium and cook, stirring frequently, for 4–5 minutes, until the onion is soft and translucent. Add the garlic and ginger purées and cook for a further 5–6 minutes, until the onion is a pale golden colour.

Add the cumin and chilli powder and cook, stirring, for 1 minute. Add the tomatoes and their juice and cook for 5–6 minutes, stirring frequently, then add the 4 tablespoons of warm water. Cook for a further 3 minutes, or until

the oil separates from the spice paste. Add the marinated meat, increase the heat slightly and cook, stirring, for 5–6 minutes, until the meat changes colour.

Add the salt and sugar, stir, then pour in the 175 ml/6 fl oz warm water. Bring to the boil, then reduce the heat to low, cover and simmer, stirring occasionally, for 55–60 minutes.

Meanwhile, blanch the spinach in a large saucepan of boiling salted water for 2 minutes, drain and immediately plunge into cold water.

Heat the ghee in a separate medium-sized saucepan over a low heat. Add the chopped garlic and cook, stirring, until the garlic is lightly browned. Stir in the nutmeg and garam masala. Squeeze out the excess water from the spinach, add to the spiced butter and stir to mix thoroughly. Add the spinach mixture to the curry, then add the cream. Stir to mix well and simmer, uncovered, for 2–3 minutes. Remove from the heat and serve immediately with Chilli-coriander Naan or plain boiled basmati rice.

# Goan fish curry

## *Caldeen*

**Serves 4**

4 skinless salmon fillets,
about 200 g/7 oz each

1 tsp salt, or to taste

1 tbsp lemon juice

3 tbsp sunflower or olive oil

1 large onion, finely chopped

2 tsp garlic purée

2 tsp ginger purée

$^1/_2$ tsp ground turmeric

1 tsp ground coriander

$^1/_2$ tsp ground cumin

$^1/_2$–1 tsp chilli powder

250 ml/9 fl oz canned coconut milk

2–3 green chillies, sliced
lengthways (deseeded if you like)

2 tbsp cider vinegar or white
wine vinegar

2 tbsp chopped fresh
coriander leaves

plain boiled basmati rice, to serve

Goa is well known for its fish and shellfish dishes, which are usually cooked in coconut milk. For this dish salmon has been chosen because its firm flesh lends itself well to curry dishes and takes on the flavours of all the spices extremely well.

Cut each salmon fillet in half and lay on a flat surface in a single layer. Sprinkle with half the salt and the lemon juice and rub in gently. Cover and leave to marinate in the refrigerator for 15–20 minutes.

Heat the oil in a frying pan over a medium heat, add the onion and cook, stirring frequently to ensure even colouring, for 8–9 minutes, until a pale golden colour.

Add the garlic and ginger purées and cook, stirring, for 1 minute, then add the turmeric, ground coriander, cumin and chilli powder and cook, stirring, for 1 minute. Add the coconut milk, chillies and vinegar, then the remaining salt, stir well and simmer, uncovered, for 6–8 minutes.

Add the fish and cook gently for 5–6 minutes. Stir in the fresh coriander and remove from the heat. Serve immediately with plain boiled basmati rice.

### Cook's tip
This curry improves in flavour if you cook it in advance and reheat very gently before serving. You can safely store it in the refrigerator for up to 48 hours.

# Pistachio chicken korma

## *Murgh korma pistadar*

**Serves 4**

115 g/4 oz shelled pistachio nuts

200 ml/7 fl oz boiling water

good pinch of saffron threads, pounded

2 tbsp hot milk

700 g/1 lb 9 oz skinless, boneless chicken breasts or thighs, cut into 2.5-cm/1-inch cubes

1 tsp salt, or to taste

1/2 tsp pepper

juice of 1/2 lemon

55 g/2 oz ghee or unsalted butter

6 green cardamom pods

1 large onion, finely chopped

2 tsp garlic purée

2 tsp ginger purée

1 tbsp ground coriander

1/2 tsp chilli powder

280 g/10 oz whole milk natural yogurt, whisked

150 ml/5 fl oz single cream

2 tbsp rosewater

6–8 white rose petals, washed, to garnish

plain boiled rice, Lemon-laced Basmati Rice (see page 72) or naan, to serve

It is a common misconception that korma is a mild and creamy dish. In fact, korma is not a dish but one of the several techniques used in Indian cooking. This delectable korma from Delhi has an unusual and irresistible aroma and taste.

Soak the pistachio nuts in the boiling water in a heatproof bowl for 20 minutes. Meanwhile, soak the pounded saffron in the hot milk.

Put the chicken in a non-reactive bowl and add the salt, pepper and lemon juice. Rub into the chicken, cover and leave to marinate in the refrigerator for 30 minutes.

Melt the ghee in a medium-sized, heavy-based saucepan over a low heat and add the cardamom pods. When they have puffed up, add the onion and increase the heat to medium. Cook, stirring frequently, for 8–9 minutes, until the onion is a pale golden colour.

Add the garlic and ginger purées and cook, stirring frequently, for a further 2–3 minutes. Add the coriander and chilli powder and cook, stirring, for 30 seconds. Add the chicken,

increase the heat to medium–high and cook, stirring constantly, for 5–6 minutes, until it changes colour.

Reduce the heat to low and add the yogurt and the saffron and milk mixture. Bring to a slow simmer, cover and cook for 15 minutes. Stir halfway through to ensure that it does not stick to the bottom of the pan.

Meanwhile, put the pistachio nuts and their soaking water in a blender or food processor and process until smooth. Add to the chicken mixture, followed by the cream. Cover and simmer, stirring occasionally, for a further 15–20 minutes. Stir in the rosewater and remove from the heat. Garnish with the rose petals and serve immediately with plain boiled rice, Lemon-laced Basmati Rice or naan.

# Chicken biryani

## *Murgh biryani*

**Serves 4-5**

85 g/3 oz whole milk natural yogurt

1 tbsp garlic purée

1 tbsp ginger purée

700 g/1 lb 9 oz boneless chicken thighs, skinned

1 tbsp white poppy seeds

2 tsp coriander seeds

1/2 mace blade

2 bay leaves, torn into small pieces

1/2 tsp black peppercorns

1 tsp green cardamom seeds

2.5-cm/1-inch piece cinnamon stick, broken up

4 cloves

55 g/2 oz ghee or unsalted butter

1 large onion, finely sliced

11/2 tsp salt, or to taste

2 tbsp sunflower oil

1 onion, finely sliced

raita, to serve

### Rice

pinch of saffron threads, pounded

2 tbsp hot milk

11/2 tsp salt

2 x 5-cm/2-inch cinnamon sticks

3 star anise

2 bay leaves, crumbled

4 cloves

4 green cardamom pods, bruised

450 g/1 lb basmati rice, washed

In this dish from the snow-fed foothills of the Himalayas, the naturally fragrant basmati rice is enhanced with cinnamon, cardamom and star anise, and layered with delicately spiced chicken. It is cooked in a sealed pot to conserve the flavours.

Put the yogurt and garlic and ginger purées in a bowl and beat together with a fork until thoroughly blended.

Put the chicken in a non-reactive bowl, add the yogurt mixture and mix until well blended. Cover and leave to marinate in the refrigerator for 2 hours.

Grind the next 8 ingredients (all the seeds and spices) to a fine powder in a coffee grinder and set aside.

In a flameproof casserole large enough to hold the chicken and the rice together, melt the ghee over a medium heat, add the onion and cook, stirring frequently, for 8–10 minutes, until a medium brown colour. Reduce the heat to low, add the ground ingredients and cook, stirring, for 2–3 minutes. Add the marinated chicken and salt and cook, stirring, for 2 minutes. Turn off the heat and keep the chicken covered.

To make the rice, soak the pounded saffron in the hot milk and set aside to soak for 20 minutes. Preheat the oven to 180°C/350°F/ Gas Mark 4.

Bring a large saucepan of water to the boil and add the salt and spices. Add the rice, return to the boil and boil steadily for 2 minutes. Drain the rice, reserving the whole spices, and pile on top of the chicken. Dot the surface of the rice with the saffron and milk, making sure that you add any remaining threads.

Soak a piece of greaseproof paper large enough to cover the top of the rice fully and squeeze out the excess water. Lay on top of the rice. Soak a clean tea towel, wring out and lay loosely on top of the greaseproof paper. Cover the casserole with a piece of foil. It is important to cover the rice in this way to contain all the steam inside the casserole, as the biryani cooks entirely in the vapour created inside the casserole. Put the lid on top and cook in the centre of the preheated oven for 1 hour. Turn off the oven and leave the rice to stand inside for 30 minutes.

Meanwhile, heat the oil in a small saucepan over a medium heat, add the onion and cook, stirring frequently, for 12–15 minutes, until well browned.

Transfer the biryani to a serving dish and garnish with the fried onions. Traditionally, biryani is eaten with raita.

# Chicken with lashings of onions

## *Murgh do piaza*

The meaning of *do piaza* remains controversial. It is widely believed to mean a dish with twice the normal amount of onions, but connoisseurs of Mogul food argue that it is a Mogul term meaning any meat or poultry cooked with vegetables.

### Serves 4

700 g/1 lb 9 oz skinless, boneless chicken breasts or thighs

juice of 1/2 lemon

1 tsp salt, or to taste

5 tbsp sunflower or olive oil

2 large onions, roughly chopped

5 large garlic cloves, roughly chopped

2.5-cm/1-inch piece fresh ginger, roughly chopped

2 tbsp whole milk natural yogurt

2.5-cm/1-inch piece cinnamon stick, halved

4 green cardamom pods, bruised

4 cloves

1/2 tsp black peppercorns

1/2 tsp ground turmeric

1/2–1 tsp chilli powder

1 tsp ground coriander

4 tbsp passata

150 ml/5 fl oz warm water

1/2 tsp granulated sugar

8 shallots, halved

1 tsp garam masala

2 tbsp chopped fresh coriander leaves

1 tomato, chopped

Indian bread, to serve

Cut the chicken into 2.5-cm/1-inch cubes and put in a non-reactive bowl. Add the lemon juice and half the salt and rub well into the chicken. Cover and leave to marinate in the refrigerator for 20 minutes.

Heat 1 tablespoon of the oil in a small saucepan over a medium heat, add the onions, garlic and ginger and cook, stirring frequently, for 4–5 minutes. Remove from the heat and leave to cool slightly. Transfer the ingredients to a blender or food processor, add the yogurt and blend to a purée.

Heat 3 tablespoons of the remaining oil in a medium-sized, heavy-based saucepan over a low heat, add the cinnamon stick, cardamom pods, cloves and peppercorns and cook, stirring, for 25–30 seconds. Add the puréed ingredients, increase the heat to medium and cook, stirring frequently, for 5 minutes.

Add the turmeric, chilli powder and ground coriander and cook, stirring, for 2 minutes. Add the passata and cook, stirring, for

3 minutes. Increase the heat slightly, then add the marinated chicken and cook, stirring, until it changes colour. Add the warm water, the remaining salt and the sugar. Bring to the boil, then reduce the heat to low, cover and cook for 10 minutes. Remove the lid and cook, uncovered, for a further 10 minutes, or until the sauce thickens. You can adjust the consistency of the sauce to your liking by reducing or increasing the cooking time at this stage.

Meanwhile, heat the remaining 1 tablespoon of oil in a small saucepan, add the shallots and stir-fry until browned and separated. Add the garam masala and cook, stirring, for 30 seconds. Stir the shallot mixture into the curry and simmer for 2 minutes. Stir in the fresh coriander and chopped tomato and remove from the heat. Serve immediately with any Indian bread.

# Chicken with stir-fried spices

## *Murgh jalfrazie*

Serves 4

700 g/1 lb 9 oz skinless, boneless chicken breasts or thighs

juice of 1/2 lemon

1 tsp salt, or to taste

5 tbsp sunflower or olive oil

1 large onion, finely chopped

2 tsp garlic purée

2 tsp ginger purée

1/2 tsp ground turmeric

1 tsp ground cumin

2 tsp ground coriander

1/2–1 tsp chilli powder

150 g/51/2 oz canned tomatoes

150 ml/5 fl oz warm water

1 large garlic clove, finely chopped

1 small or 1/2 large red pepper, deseeded and cut into 2.5-cm/ 1-inch pieces

1 small or 1/2 large green pepper, deseeded and cut into 2.5-cm/ 1-inch pieces

1 tsp garam masala

Indian bread or plain boiled basmati rice, to serve

The popular jalfrazie was created during the British Raj to use up cold cooked meat. This recipe comes from Kolkatta (previously Calcutta), where jalfrazie was served frequently to the members of the East India Company.

Cut the chicken into 2.5-cm/1-inch cubes and put in a non-reactive bowl. Add the lemon juice and half the salt and rub well into the chicken. Cover and leave to marinate in the refrigerator for 20 minutes.

Heat 4 tablespoons of the oil in a medium-sized, heavy-based saucepan over a medium heat. Add the onion and cook, stirring frequently, for 8–9 minutes, until lightly browned. Add the garlic and ginger purées and cook, stirring, for 3 minutes. Add the turmeric, cumin, coriander and chilli powder and cook, stirring, for 1 minute. Add the tomatoes and their juice and cook for 2–3 minutes, stirring frequently, until the oil separates from the spice paste.

Add the marinated chicken, increase the heat slightly and cook, stirring, until it changes colour. Add the warm water and the remaining salt. Bring to the boil, then reduce the heat, cover and simmer for 25 minutes.

Heat the remaining 1 tablespoon of oil in a small saucepan or frying pan over a low heat. Add the chopped garlic and cook, stirring frequently, until browned. Add the peppers, increase the heat to medium and stir-fry for 2 minutes, then stir in the garam masala. Fold the pepper mixture into the curry. Remove from the heat and serve immediately with Indian bread or plain boiled basmati rice.

# Pork curry with chilli, garlic and vinegar

## *Vindaloo*

**Serves 4**

2–6 dried red chillies (long slim variety), torn into 2–3 pieces

5 cloves

2.5-cm/1-inch piece cinnamon stick, broken up

4 cardamom pods

1/2 tsp black peppercorns

1/2 mace blade

1/4 nutmeg, lightly crushed

1 tsp cumin seeds

1 1/2 tsp coriander seeds

1/2 tsp fenugreek seeds

2 tsp garlic purée

1 tbsp ginger purée

3 tbsp cider vinegar or white wine vinegar

1 tbsp tamarind juice or juice of 1/2 lime

700 g/1 lb 9 oz boned leg of pork, cut into 2.5-cm/1-inch cubes

4 tbsp sunflower or olive oil, plus 2 tsp

2 large onions, finely chopped

250 ml/9 fl oz warm water, plus 4 tbsp

1 tsp salt, or to taste

1 tsp soft dark brown sugar

2 large garlic cloves, finely sliced

8–10 curry leaves, fresh or dried

*To serve*

plain boiled basmati rice

vegetable side dish

The name *vindaloo* is derived from two Portuguese words: *vin*, meaning 'vinegar', and *alho*, meaning 'garlic'. When the Portuguese travelled to India, they took pork preserved in vinegar, garlic and pepper, which was spiced up to suit Indian tastes!

Grind the first 10 ingredients (all the spices) to a fine powder in a coffee grinder. Transfer the ground spices to a bowl and add the garlic and ginger purées, vinegar and tamarind juice. Mix together to form a paste.

Put the pork in a large, non-reactive bowl and rub about one-quarter of the spice paste into the meat. Cover and leave to marinate in the refrigerator for 30–40 minutes.

Heat the 4 tablespoons of oil in a medium-sized, heavy-based saucepan over a medium heat, add the onions and cook, stirring frequently, for 8–10 minutes, until lightly browned. Add the remaining spice paste and cook, stirring constantly, for 5–6 minutes. Add 2 tablespoons of warm water and cook until it evaporates. Repeat with the other 2 tablespoons of water.

Add the marinated pork and cook over a medium–high heat for 5–6 minutes, until the meat changes colour. Add the salt, sugar and the remaining 250 ml/9 fl oz warm water. Bring to the boil, then reduce the heat to low, cover and simmer for 50–55 minutes, until the meat is tender.

Meanwhile, heat the 2 teaspoons of oil in a very small saucepan or a steel ladle over a low heat. Add the sliced garlic and cook, stirring frequently, until it begins to brown. Add the curry leaves and leave to sizzle for 15–20 seconds. Stir the garlic mixture into the vindaloo. Remove from the heat and serve immediately with plain boiled basmati rice and a vegetable side dish.

# Prawns in coconut milk with chilli and curry leaves

## *Prawn pappas*

**Serves 4**

4 tbsp sunflower or olive oil

1/2 tsp black or brown mustard seeds

1/2 tsp fenugreek seeds

1 large onion, finely chopped

2 tsp garlic purée

2 tsp ginger purée

1–2 green chillies, chopped (deseeded if you like)

1 tbsp ground coriander

1/2 tsp ground turmeric

1/2 tsp chilli powder

1 tsp salt, or to taste

250 ml/9 fl oz canned coconut milk

450 g/1 lb cooked peeled tiger prawns, thawed and drained if frozen

1 tbsp tamarind juice or juice of 1/2 lime

1/2 tsp crushed black peppercorns

10–12 curry leaves, fresh or dried

*To serve*

plain boiled basmati rice

vegetable side dish

This chilli-hot, turmeric-tinged prawn curry is mellowed with coconut milk and distinctively flavoured with curry leaves, which are available fresh in Asian shops and dried in large supermarkets. Fresh ones can be frozen for up to three months.

Heat 3 tablespoons of the oil in a medium-sized saucepan over a medium–high heat. When hot but not smoking, add the mustard seeds, followed by the fenugreek seeds and the onion. Cook, stirring frequently, for 5–6 minutes, until the onion is soft but not brown. Add the garlic and ginger purées and the chillies and cook, stirring frequently, for a further 5–6 minutes, until the onion is a light golden colour.

Add the coriander, turmeric and chilli powder and cook, stirring, for 1 minute. Add the salt and coconut milk, followed by the prawns and tamarind juice. Bring to a slow simmer and cook, stirring occasionally, for 3–4 minutes.

Meanwhile, heat the remaining 1 tablespoon of oil in a very small saucepan or a steel ladle over a medium heat. Add the peppercorns and curry leaves. Turn off the heat and leave to sizzle for 20–25 seconds, then fold the aromatic oil into the prawn mixture. Remove from the heat and serve immediately with plain boiled basmati rice and a vegetable side dish.

# Garden peas and Indian cheese in chilli-tomato sauce

## *Mutter paneer*

**Serves 4**

4 tbsp sunflower or olive oil

250 g/9 oz paneer, cut into
2.5-cm/1-inch cubes

4 green cardamom pods, bruised

2 bay leaves

1 onion, finely chopped

2 tsp garlic purée

2 tsp ginger purée

2 tsp ground coriander

1/2 tsp ground turmeric

1/2–1 tsp chilli powder

150 g/5½ oz canned chopped
tomatoes

425 ml/15 fl oz warm water,
plus 2 tbsp

1 tsp salt, or to taste

125 g/4½ oz frozen peas

1/2 tsp garam masala

2 tbsp single cream

2 tbsp chopped fresh coriander
leaves

Chilli-coriander Naan (see page 76)
or other Indian bread, to serve

Paneer, or Indian cheese, is a great source of protein for the vast majority of the Indian population who don't eat meat. This is a traditional vegetarian main course where tender morsels of paneer are simmered in a spice-infused tomato sauce.

Heat 2 tablespoons of the oil in a medium-sized, non-stick saucepan over a medium heat. Add the paneer and cook, stirring frequently, for 3–4 minutes, or until evenly browned. Paneer tends to splatter in hot oil, so stand slightly away from the hob. Alternatively, use a splatter screen. Remove and drain on kitchen paper.

Add the remaining oil to the saucepan and reduce the heat to low. Add the cardamom pods and bay leaves and leave to sizzle gently for 20–25 seconds. Add the onion, increase the heat to medium and cook, stirring frequently, for 4–5 minutes, until the onion is soft. Add the garlic and ginger purées and cook, stirring frequently, for a further 3–4 minutes, until the onion is a pale golden colour.

Add the ground coriander, turmeric and chilli powder and cook, stirring, for 1 minute. Add the tomatoes and their juice and cook, stirring frequently, for 4–5 minutes. Add the 2 tablespoons of warm water and cook, stirring frequently, for 3 minutes, or until the oil separates from the spice paste.

Add the remaining warm water and salt. Bring to the boil, then reduce the heat to low and simmer, uncovered, for 7–8 minutes.

Add the paneer and peas and simmer for 5 minutes. Stir in the garam masala, cream and fresh coriander and remove from the heat. Serve immediately with Chilli-coriander Naan or any other Indian bread.

# Vegetable korma

## Subzion ka korma

Serves 4

85 g/3 oz cashew nuts

175 ml/6 fl oz boiling water

good pinch of saffron threads, pounded

2 tbsp hot milk

1 small cauliflower, divided into 1-cm/1/2-inch florets

115 g/4 oz green beans, cut into 2.5-cm/1-inch lengths

115 g/4 oz carrots, cut into 2.5-cm/1-inch sticks

250 g/9 oz new potatoes, boiled in their skins and cooled

4 tbsp sunflower or olive oil

1 large onion, finely chopped

2 tsp ginger purée

1–2 green chillies, chopped (deseeded if you like)

2 tsp ground coriander

1/2 tsp ground turmeric

6 tbsp warm water

400 ml/14 fl oz good-quality vegetable stock

1/2 tsp salt, or to taste

2 tbsp single cream

2 tsp ghee or butter

1 tsp garam masala

1/4 tsp grated nutmeg

Lemon-laced Basmati Rice, to serve (see page 72)

The korma style of cooking was originally used only for meat and poultry. However, its popularity is so overwhelming that various vegetarian recipes have been created in recent years. The dish is a subtle sensation of flavours and a total visual delight.

Soak the cashew nuts in the boiling water in a heatproof bowl for 20 minutes. Meanwhile, soak the pounded saffron in the hot milk.

Blanch the vegetables, one at a time, in a saucepan of boiling salted water: blanch the cauliflower for 3 minutes, drain and immediately plunge in cold water; blanch the green beans for 3 minutes, drain and plunge in cold water; and blanch the carrots for 4 minutes, drain and plunge in cold water. Peel the potatoes, if you like, and halve or quarter them according to their size.

Heat the oil in a medium-sized, heavy-based saucepan over a medium heat. Add the onion, ginger purée and chillies and cook, stirring frequently, for 5–6 minutes, until the onion is soft. Add the coriander and turmeric and cook, stirring, for 1 minute. Add 3 tablespoons of the warm water and cook for 2–3 minutes. Repeat this process once more, then cook, stirring frequently, for 2–3 minutes, or until the oil separates from the spice paste.

Add the stock, saffron and milk mixture and salt, and bring to the boil. Drain the vegetables, add to the saucepan and return to the boil. Reduce the heat to low and simmer for 2–3 minutes.

Meanwhile, put the cashew nuts and their soaking water in a food processor and process until well blended. Add to the korma, then stir in the cream. Leave over a very low heat while you prepare the final seasoning.

Melt the ghee in a very small saucepan or a steel ladle over a low heat. Add the garam masala and nutmeg and leave the spices to sizzle gently for 20–25 seconds. Fold the spiced butter into the korma. Remove from the heat and serve immediately with Lemon-laced Basmati Rice.

### Cook's tip

You can store this korma in the refrigerator for 3–4 days, but reheat very gently, adding a little warm water to maintain the consistency of the sauce.

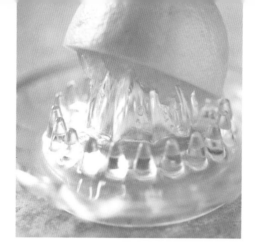

# Chickpeas in coconut milk

## *Vatana gashi*

From the palm-fringed southern coastal area of India, where coconut milk is used as an everyday stock, this is a simple but delicious dish. Traditionally, dried chickpeas would be used, but canned chickpeas are a quick and easy alternative.

**Serves 4**

275 g/9³⁄4 oz potatoes, cut into 1-cm/¹⁄2-inch cubes

250 ml/9 fl oz hot water

400 g/14 oz canned chickpeas, drained and well rinsed

250 ml/9 fl oz canned coconut milk

1 tsp salt, or to taste

2 tbsp sunflower or olive oil

4 large garlic cloves, finely chopped or crushed

2 tsp ground coriander

¹⁄2 tsp ground turmeric

¹⁄2–1 tsp chilli powder

juice of ¹⁄2 lemon

Indian bread or plain boiled basmati rice, to serve

Put the potatoes in a medium-sized saucepan and pour in the hot water. Bring to the boil, then reduce the heat to low and cook, covered, for 6–7 minutes, until the potatoes are al dente. Add the chickpeas and cook, uncovered, for 3–4 minutes, until the potatoes are tender. Add the coconut milk and salt and bring to a slow simmer.

Meanwhile, heat the oil in a small saucepan over a low heat. Add the garlic and cook, stirring frequently, until it begins to brown.

Add the coriander, turmeric and chilli powder and cook, stirring, for 25–30 seconds. Fold the aromatic oil into the chickpeas. Stir in the lemon juice and remove from the heat. Serve immediately with any Indian bread or plain boiled basmati rice.

### Cook's tip
You can use green beans or a mixture of green beans and carrots instead of the potatoes. Black-eyed beans are also excellent for this recipe.

# Side Dishes

When an Indian meal is served, the side dishes often steal the show, since they are so varied and enticing in taste, texture and colour. Rich main courses should be teamed with simply spiced side dishes, while substantial side dishes combine well with relatively plain main courses.

Alongside classic vegetable pairings such as new potatoes with spinach and okra with onions, this section features the well-loved lentil dish *tarka dhal*, as well as tangy chutneys – perfect with Indian snacks – and *raita*, the cooling favourite. Delicately spiced basmati rice dishes and different breads are also included here, and are ideal for serving with any of the main dishes in the book.

# Garlic and chilli-flavoured potatoes with cauliflower

## *Aloo gobi*

Serves 4

350 g/12 oz new potatoes

1 small cauliflower

2 tbsp sunflower or olive oil

1 tsp black or brown mustard seeds

1 tsp cumin seeds

5 large garlic cloves, lightly crushed, then chopped

1–2 green chillies, finely chopped (deseeded if you like)

$1/2$ tsp ground turmeric

$1/2$ tsp salt, or to taste

2 tbsp chopped fresh coriander leaves

Aloo gobi is a well-known and popular dish in most Indian restaurants. There are as many different versions as there are cooks. This version is easy to make, can be part-prepared ahead of time and is deliciously moreish!

Cook the potatoes in their skins in a saucepan of boiling water for 20 minutes, or until tender. Drain, then soak in cold water for 30 minutes. Peel them, if you like, then halve or quarter according to their size – they should be only slightly bigger than the size of the cauliflower florets (see below).

Meanwhile, divide the cauliflower into about 1-cm/$1/2$-inch diameter florets and blanch in a large saucepan of boiling salted water for 3 minutes. Drain and plunge into iced water to prevent further cooking, then drain again.

Heat the oil in a medium-sized saucepan over a medium heat. When hot but not smoking, add the mustard seeds, then the cumin seeds.

Remove from the heat and add the garlic and chillies. Return to a low heat and cook, stirring, until the garlic has a light brown tinge.

Stir in the turmeric, followed by the cauliflower and the potatoes. Add the salt, increase the heat slightly and cook, stirring, until the vegetables are well blended with the spices and heated through.

Stir in the coriander, remove from the heat and serve immediately to accompany any Indian main course dish with rice or bread.

# New potatoes with spiced spinach

## *Saag aloo*

**Serves 4**

350 g/12 oz new potatoes

250 g/9 oz spinach leaves, thawed if frozen

3 tbsp sunflower or olive oil

1 large onion, finely sliced

1 green chilli, finely chopped (deseeded if you like)

2 tsp garlic purée

2 tsp ginger purée

1 tsp ground coriander

1/2 tsp ground cumin

1/2 tsp chilli powder

1/2 tsp ground turmeric

200 g/7 oz canned chopped tomatoes

1/2 tsp granulated sugar

1 tsp salt, or to taste

3 tbsp single cream

This traditional and popular dish is easy to make and is a perfect accompaniment to most Indian meals. Generally, fresh spinach leaves are blanched and puréed, but you can use frozen puréed spinach, which cuts down on preparation time.

Cook the potatoes in their skins in a saucepan of boiling water for 20 minutes, or until tender. Drain, then soak in cold water for 30 minutes. Peel them, if you like, then halve or quarter according to their size.

Meanwhile, blanch the spinach in a large saucepan of boiling salted water for 2 minutes, then drain. Transfer to a blender or food processor and blend to a purée. Set aside.

Heat 2 tablespoons of the oil in a medium-sized saucepan over a medium heat. Add the onion and cook, stirring frequently, for 10–12 minutes, until well browned, reducing the heat to low for the last 2–3 minutes. Remove from the heat and remove the excess oil from the onion by pressing against the side of the saucepan with a wooden spoon. Remove and drain on kitchen paper.

Return the pan to the heat, add the remaining oil and heat. Add the chilli and garlic and ginger purées and cook over a low heat, stirring, for 2–3 minutes. Add the coriander, cumin, chilli powder and turmeric and cook, stirring, for 1 minute. Add the tomatoes and their juice, increase the heat to medium and add the sugar. Cook, stirring frequently, for 5–6 minutes, until the tomatoes have reached a paste-like consistency.

Add the potatoes, spinach, salt and fried onions and cook, stirring, for 2–3 minutes. Stir in the cream and cook for 1 minute. Remove from the heat and serve immediately with any curry.

# Mushrooms in a rich tomato and onion sauce

## Mushroom bhaji

**Serves 4**

280 g/10 oz closed-cup white mushrooms

4 tbsp sunflower or olive oil

1 onion, finely chopped

1 green chilli, finely chopped (deseeded if you like)

2 tsp garlic purée

1 tsp ground cumin

1 tsp ground coriander

1/2 tsp chilli powder

1/2 tsp salt, or to taste

1 tbsp tomato purée

3 tbsp water

1 tbsp snipped fresh chives

Mushroom bhaji is not a traditional Indian dish, but mushrooms do seem to have a certain affinity with a spiced tomato-based sauce. It is important to choose the right combination of spices in order to complement the natural taste of the mushrooms.

Wipe the mushrooms with damp kitchen paper and slice thickly.

Heat the oil in a medium-sized saucepan over a medium heat. Add the onion and chilli and cook, stirring frequently, for 5–6 minutes, until the onion is soft but not brown. Add the garlic purée and cook, stirring, for 2 minutes.

Add the cumin, coriander and chilli powder and cook, stirring, for 1 minute. Add the mushrooms, salt and tomato purée and stir until all the ingredients are thoroughly blended.

Sprinkle the water evenly over the mushrooms and reduce the heat to low. Cover and cook for 10 minutes, stirring halfway through. The sauce should have thickened, but if it appears runny, cook, uncovered, for 3–4 minutes, or until you achieve the desired consistency.

Transfer to a serving dish, sprinkle the chives on top and serve immediately.

# Okra stir-fried with onions

## *Bhindi-piaz*

**Serves 4**

280 g/10 oz okra

1 small red pepper

1 onion

2 tbsp sunflower or olive oil

1 tsp black or brown mustard seeds

1/2 tsp cumin seeds

3 large garlic cloves, lightly crushed, then chopped

1/2 tsp chilli powder

1/2 tsp salt, or to taste

1/2 tsp garam masala

plain boiled basmati rice, to serve

Okra stir-fried with onions and spices makes a superb side dish. Here, the combination of the soft green okra, bright red pepper and white onion, all dotted with black mustard seeds, creates a colourful, appetizing effect.

Scrub each okra gently, rinse well in cold running water, then slice off the hard head. Halve diagonally and set aside.

Remove the seeds and core from the red pepper and cut into 4-cm/1-inch strips. Halve the onion lengthways and cut into 5-mm/1/4-inch thick slices.

Heat the oil in a heavy-based frying pan or wok over a medium heat. When hot but not smoking, add the mustard seeds, followed by the cumin seeds. Remove from the heat and add the garlic. Return to a low heat and cook the garlic gently, stirring, for 1 minute, or until lightly browned.

Add the okra, red pepper and onion, increase the heat to medium–high and stir-fry for 2 minutes. Add the chilli powder and salt and stir-fry for a further 3 minutes. Add the garam masala and stir-fry for 1 minute. Remove from the heat and serve immediately with plain boiled basmati rice.

### Cook's tip

Make sure that the oil is at the right temperature or else the mustard seeds will not release their delightful nutty taste. To test the temperature, drop 1–2 mustard seeds into the hot oil – if they pop straight away, the oil is just right.

# Lentils with cumin and shallots

## *Tarka dhal*

The word *tarka* means 'tempering'. Tarka dhal is easy to cook, as the boiled dhal is simply tempered with a few whole spices, and either onion (or in this case shallot) or garlic is added to the hot oil before being folded into the cooked lentils.

**Serves 4**

200 g/7 oz red split lentils

850 ml/1 1/2 pints water

1 tsp salt, or to taste

2 tsp sunflower or olive oil

1/2 tsp black or brown mustard seeds

1/2 tsp cumin seeds

4 shallots, finely chopped

2 green chillies, chopped (deseeded if you like)

1 tsp ground turmeric

1 tsp ground cumin

1 fresh tomato, chopped

2 tbsp chopped fresh coriander leaves

Lemon-laced Basmati Rice (see page 72) or naan, to serve

Wash the lentils until the water runs clear and put into a medium-sized saucepan. Add the water and bring to the boil. Reduce the heat to medium and skim off the froth. Cook, uncovered, for 10 minutes. Reduce the heat to low, cover and cook for 45 minutes, stirring occasionally to ensure that the lentils do not stick to the bottom of the pan as they thicken. Stir in the salt.

Meanwhile, heat the oil in a small saucepan over a medium heat. When hot but not smoking, add the mustard seeds, followed by the cumin seeds. Add the shallots and chillies and cook, stirring, for 2–3 minutes, then add the turmeric and ground cumin. Add the tomato and cook, stirring, for 30 seconds.

Fold the shallot mixture into the cooked lentils. Stir in the coriander, remove from the heat and serve immediately with Lemon-laced Basmati Rice or naan.

### Cook's tip

If you add salt to the lentils too soon, they will take longer to cook.

# Cucumber in spiced yogurt

## *Kheeva ka raita*

1 small cucumber

175 g/6 oz whole milk natural yogurt

1/4 tsp granulated sugar

1/4 tsp salt

1 tsp cumin seeds

10–12 black peppercorns

1/4 tsp paprika

Raita is a generic name for any salad with a spiced yogurt dressing. In the north of India, the yogurt is flavoured with roasted crushed cumin seeds and chilli, while southern India excels in making a yogurt dressing with a hot oil seasoning.

Peel the cucumber and scoop out the seeds. Cut the flesh into bite-sized pieces and set aside.

Put the yogurt in a bowl and beat with a fork until smooth. Add the sugar and salt and mix well.

Preheat a small, heavy-based saucepan over a medium–high heat. When the pan is hot, turn off the heat and add the cumin seeds and peppercorns. Stir around for 40–50 seconds, until they release their aroma. Remove from the pan and leave to cool for 5 minutes, then crush in a mortar with a pestle or on a hard surface with a rolling pin.

Reserve 1/4 teaspoon of this mixture and stir the remainder into the yogurt. Add the cucumber and stir to mix.

Transfer the raita to a serving dish and sprinkle with the reserved toasted spices and the paprika.

### Cook's tip

To add an extra dimension to the taste and texture of the raita, crush 55 g/2 oz roasted salted peanuts. Mix half into the raita and sprinkle the remainder on top just before serving.

# Mint and spinach chutney

## Pudina-palak ki chutney

Serves 4-6

55 g/2 oz tender fresh spinach leaves

3 tbsp fresh mint leaves

2 tbsp chopped fresh coriander leaves

1 small red onion, roughly chopped

1 small garlic clove, chopped

1 green chilli, chopped (deseeded if you like)

2$\frac{1}{2}$ tsp granulated sugar

1 tbsp tamarind juice or juice of $\frac{1}{2}$ lemon

Chutneys and raitas are an integral part of an Indian meal. Snacks and starters such as samosas, onion bhajiyas and tikkas are always accompanied by an array of mouth-watering chutneys. This chutney tastes wonderful yet it is so simple to make.

Put all the ingredients in a blender or food processor and blend until smooth, adding only as much water as necessary to enable the blades to move.

Transfer to a serving bowl, cover and chill in the refrigerator for at least 30 minutes before serving.

### Cook's tip
If you like the refreshing mint and coriander dip served in Indian restaurants, mix a tablespoonful of this chutney with 125 g/ 4$\frac{1}{2}$ oz whole milk natural yogurt. Taste and adjust the seasoning if necessary.

# Mint and coriander rice with toasted pine kernels

## *Pudina-dhania ka chawal*

Serves 4

good pinch of saffron threads, pounded

2 tbsp hot milk

225 g/8 oz basmati rice

2 tbsp sunflower or olive oil

5-cm/2-inch piece cinnamon stick, broken in half

4 green cardamom pods, bruised

2 star anise

2 bay leaves

450 ml/16 fl oz lukewarm water

3 tbsp fresh coriander leaves, finely chopped

2 tbsp fresh mint leaves, finely chopped, or 1 tsp dried mint

1 tsp salt, or to taste

25 g /1 oz pine kernels

The slender grains of fragrant basmati rice complement the delicately flavoured pine kernels, both prized ingredients from northern India, in this sumptuous pilau. Saffron adds an exotic touch, with its age-old reputation for being rare and costly.

Soak the pounded saffron threads in the hot milk and set aside until you are ready to use.

Wash the rice in several changes of cold water until the water runs clear. Leave to soak in fresh cold water for 20 minutes, then leave to drain in a colander.

Heat the oil in a medium-sized, heavy-based saucepan over a low heat. Add the cinnamon, cardamom, star anise and bay leaves and leave to sizzle gently for 20–25 seconds. Add the rice and stir well to ensure that the grains are coated with the flavoured oil.

Add the water, stir once and bring to the boil. Add the saffron and milk, coriander, mint and salt and boil for 2–3 minutes. Cover tightly, reduce the heat to very low and cook for 7–8 minutes. Turn off the heat and leave to stand, covered, for 7–8 minutes.

Meanwhile, preheat a small, heavy-based frying pan over a medium heat, add the pine kernels and cook, stirring, until they begin to glisten with their natural oils and are lightly toasted. Alternatively, cook in a foil-covered grill pan under a preheated medium grill, turning 2–3 times, until lightly toasted. Transfer to a plate and leave to cool.

Add half the toasted pine kernels to the rice and fluff up the rice with a fork. Transfer to a serving dish, garnish with the remaining pine kernels and serve immediately.

# Lemon-laced basmati rice

## *Nimbu chawal*

**Serves 4**

225 g/8 oz basmati rice

2 tbsp sunflower or olive oil

1/2 tsp black or brown mustard
seeds

10–12 curry leaves, preferably fresh

25 g/1 oz cashew nuts

1/4 tsp ground turmeric

1 tsp salt, or to taste

450 ml/16 fl oz hot water

2 tbsp lemon juice

1 tbsp snipped fresh chives,
to garnish

In this much-loved dish from southern India, the snow-white grains of basmati rice are tinged with turmeric and adorned with black mustard seeds. The main flavour here is that of curry leaves, which is the hallmark of southern Indian cuisine.

Wash the rice in several changes of cold water until the water runs clear. Leave to soak in fresh cold water for 20 minutes, then leave to drain in a colander.

Heat the oil in a non-stick saucepan over a medium heat. When hot but not smoking, add the mustard seeds, followed by the curry leaves and the cashew nuts (in that order).

Stir in the turmeric, quickly followed by the rice and salt. Cook, stirring, for 1 minute, then add the hot water and lemon juice. Stir once, bring to the boil and boil for 2 minutes. Cover tightly,

reduce the heat to very low and cook for 8 minutes. Turn off the heat and leave to stand, covered, for 6–7 minutes. Fork through the rice and transfer to a serving dish. Garnish with the chives and serve immediately.

### Cook's tip
It is important to allow the cooked rice to stand to enable the grains to absorb any remaining moisture. Use a metal spoon to transfer the rice to the serving dish, as a wooden spoon will squash the delicate grains.

# Griddle-roasted flat bread

## *Chapatti*

**Makes 16**

400 g/14 oz chapatti flour (atta), plus extra for dusting

1 tsp salt

1/2 tsp granulated sugar

2 tbsp sunflower or olive oil

250 ml/9 fl oz lukewarm water

In Indian homes, chapattis are made fresh every day, using a special flour known as *atta*. Asian stores sell atta, but you can substitute a fine, wholemeal bread flour combined with plain flour, at a ratio of two-thirds wholemeal to one-third plain.

Mix the chapatti flour, salt and sugar together in a large bowl. Add the oil and work well into the flour mixture with your fingertips. Gradually add the water, mixing at the same time. When the dough is formed, transfer to a work surface and knead for 4–5 minutes. The dough is ready when all the excess moisture is absorbed by the flour. Alternatively, mix the dough in a food processor. Wrap the dough in clingfilm and leave to rest for 30 minutes.

Divide the dough in half, then cut each half into 8 equal-sized pieces. Form each piece into a ball and flatten into a round cake. Dust each cake lightly in the flour and roll out to a 15-cm/6-inch round. Keep the remaining cakes covered while you are working on one. The chapattis will cook better when freshly rolled out, so roll out and cook one at a time.

Preheat a heavy-based cast-iron griddle (tawa) or a large, heavy-based frying pan over a medium–high heat. Put a chapatti on the griddle and cook for 30 seconds. Using a thin spatula or fish slice, turn over and cook until bubbles begin to appear on the surface. Turn over again. Press the edges down gently with a clean cloth to encourage the chapatti to puff up – they will not always puff up, but this doesn't matter. Cook until brown patches appear on the underside. Remove from the pan and keep hot by wrapping in a piece of foil lined with kitchen paper. Repeat with the remaining dough cakes.

# Chilli-coriander naan

## *Mirch-dhania ke naan*

*Naan* came to India with the ancient Persians, and it means 'bread' in their language. Naan is traditionally made in the *tandoor* (Indian clay oven), but this can be emulated by using a very hot grill.

Makes 8

450 g/1 lb plain flour

2 tsp sugar

1 tsp salt

1 tsp baking powder

1 egg

250 ml/9 fl oz milk

2 tbsp sunflower or olive oil, plus extra for brushing

2 fresh red chillies, chopped (deseeded if you like)

15 g/½ oz fresh coriander leaves, chopped

2 tbsp butter, melted

Sift the flour, sugar, salt and baking powder together into a large bowl. Whisk the egg and milk together and gradually add to the flour, mixing it with a wooden spoon, until a dough is formed.

Transfer the dough to a work surface, make a depression in the centre of the dough and add the oil. Knead for 3–4 minutes, until the oil is absorbed by the flour and you have a smooth and pliable dough. Wrap the dough in clingfilm and leave to rest for 1 hour.

Divide the dough into 8 equal-sized pieces, form each piece into a ball and flatten into a thick cake. Cover the dough cakes with clingfilm and leave to rest for 10–15 minutes.

Preheat the grill on high for 10 minutes, line a grill pan with a piece of foil and brush with oil.

The traditional shape of naan is teardrop, but you can make them any shape you wish. To make the traditional shape, roll each flattened cake into a 12.5-cm/5-inch diameter round and pull the lower end gently. Carefully roll out again, maintaining the teardrop shape, to about 23 cm/9 inches in diameter. Alternatively, roll the flattened cakes out to 23-cm/9-inch rounds.

Mix the chillies and coriander together, then divide into 8 equal portions and spread each on the surface of a naan. Press gently so that the mixture sticks to the dough. Transfer a naan to the prepared grill pan and cook 13 cm/ 5 inches below the heat source for 1 minute, or until slightly puffed and brown patches appear on the surface. Watch carefully, and as soon as brown spots appear on the surface, turn over and cook the other side for 45–50 seconds, until lightly browned. Remove from the grill and brush with the melted butter. Wrap in a tea towel while you cook the remaining naans.

# Desserts

Serving an elaborate dessert is not an everyday practice in India. Fresh fruits are a popular way to end a meal, their fresh, tangy flavours offering a refreshing contrast to the spiciness of the previous courses. However, India does have a dazzling variety of sweets and desserts that are reserved for special occasions, and these differ from region to region.

A selection of the most popular Indian desserts is featured in this section, such as the sumptuous iced *kulfi* flavoured with mango; a creamy rice dish perfumed with rosewater and cardamom; and a rich fudge-like sweet made from carrots cooked in milk and enriched with nuts. As with a starter, be sure to choose a dessert that complements the main course.

# Mango-flavoured iced dessert

## *Aam ki kulfi*

**Serves 6-8**

375 g/13 oz canned evaporated milk

300 ml/10 fl oz single cream

25 g/1 oz ground almonds

115–140 g/4–5 oz granulated sugar

450 g/1 lb mango purée

1 tsp freshly ground cardamom seeds

25 g/1 oz shelled unsalted pistachio nuts, to decorate

*Kulfi* is a dairy-based dessert flavoured with fruits and nuts. Traditionally, it is made by reducing a large volume of milk to the consistency of condensed milk. This recipe is less labour-intensive, using evaporated milk and single cream.

Pour the evaporated milk and cream into a heavy-based saucepan and stir to mix. Put over a medium heat. Mix the ground almonds and sugar together, then add to the milk mixture. Cook, stirring, for 6–8 minutes, until the mixture thickens slightly.

Remove from the heat and leave the mixture to cool completely, stirring from time to time to stop a skin forming. When completely cold, stir in the mango purée and ground cardamom.

Meanwhile, preheat a small saucepan over a medium heat, add the pistachio nuts and toast for 2–3 minutes. Leave to cool, then lightly crush. Store in an airtight container until required.

Kulfi is set in traditional conical-shaped plastic or steel moulds, which you can buy from Asian stores, but you can use decorative individual jelly moulds or ice lolly moulds instead. Fill the containers of your choice with the kulfi mixture and freeze for 5–6 hours. Traditional moulds hold about 2 tablespoons of the kulfi mixture, but you can use larger containers if you like. Transfer the kulfi to the refrigerator for 40 minutes, then cut into portions with a sharp knife. Serve sprinkled with the crushed pistachio nuts to decorate.

### Cook's tip
Brush the bottom of the saucepan with a little melted butter or oil before mixing the milk and cream. This prevents the mixture from sticking.

# Indian rice dessert

## *Firni*

**Serves 4**

good pinch of saffron threads, pounded

2 tbsp hot milk

40 g/1½ oz ghee or unsalted butter

55 g/2 oz ground rice

25 g/1 oz flaked almonds

25 g/1 oz seedless raisins

600 ml/1 pint milk

450 ml/16 fl oz evaporated milk

55 g/2 oz caster sugar

12 ready-to-eat dried apricots, sliced

1 tsp freshly ground cardamom seeds

½ tsp freshly grated nutmeg

2 tbsp rosewater

*To decorate*

25 g/1 oz walnut pieces

15 g/½ oz shelled unsalted pistachio nuts

This is a hugely popular north Indian dessert, where ground rice is cooked in thickened milk with apricots, raisins, almonds and pistachio nuts, with the exotic aroma of rosewater and cardamom. It is best served chilled.

Place the pounded saffron in the hot milk and leave to soak until needed.

Reserve 2 teaspoons of the ghee and melt the remainder in a heavy-based saucepan over a low heat. Add the ground rice, almonds and raisins and cook, stirring, for 2 minutes. Add the milk, increase the heat to medium and cook, stirring, until it begins to bubble gently. Reduce the heat to low and cook, stirring frequently, for 10–12 minutes, to prevent the mixture from sticking to the bottom of the pan.

Add the evaporated milk, sugar and apricots, reserving a few slices to decorate. Cook, stirring, until the mixture thickens to the consistency of a pouring custard.

Add the cardamom, nutmeg and rosewater, stir to distribute well and remove from the heat. Leave to cool, then cover and chill in the refrigerator for at least 2 hours.

Melt the reserved ghee in a small saucepan over a low heat. Add the walnuts and cook, stirring, until they brown a little. Remove and drain on kitchen paper. Brown the pistachio nuts in the remaining ghee in the saucepan, remove and drain on kitchen paper. Leave the pistachio nuts to cool, then lightly crush.

Serve the dessert decorated with the fried nuts and the reserved apricot slices.

# Soft carrot fudge

## Gajjar ka halwa

This delicious dessert is made by cooking grated carrots in thickened milk to a soft, fudge-like consistency. A variety of contrasts in taste and texture is created by adding raisins, mixed nuts, cardamom, nutmeg and rosewater.

**Serves 4–6**

55 g/2 oz ghee or unsalted butter

2.5-cm/1-inch piece cinnamon stick, halved

25 g/1 oz flaked almonds

25 g/1 oz cashew nuts

25 g /1 oz seedless raisins

450 g/1 lb grated carrots

600 ml/1 pint milk

125 g/4 1/2 oz caster sugar

1/2 tsp freshly ground cardamom seeds

1/2 tsp freshly grated nutmeg

50 ml/2 fl oz double cream

2 tbsp rosewater

vanilla ice cream or whipped double cream, to serve

Melt the ghee in a heavy-based saucepan over a low heat. Add the cinnamon stick and leave to sizzle gently for 25–30 seconds. Add the almonds and cashew nuts and cook, stirring, until lightly browned. Remove about a dessertspoon of the nuts and reserve.

Add the raisins, carrots, milk and sugar to the saucepan, increase the heat to medium and bring the milk to boiling point. Continue to cook over a low–medium heat for 15–20 minutes, until the milk evaporates completely, stirring frequently, and scraping and blending in any thickened milk that sticks to the side of the saucepan. Don't allow any milk that is stuck to the side to brown or burn, as this will give the dessert an unpleasant flavour.

Stir in the cardamom, nutmeg, cream and rosewater. Remove from the heat and leave to cool slightly, then serve topped with a scoop of vanilla ice cream or whipped double cream. Sprinkle the reserved nuts on top of the ice cream or cream to decorate.

# Sweet saffron rice with caramelized pineapple

## Ananas ka muzzafar

Serves 4-6

good pinch of saffron threads, pounded

2 tbsp hot milk

175 g/6 oz basmati rice

1/2 fresh pineapple (225 g/8 oz prepared weight)

55 g/2 oz ghee or unsalted butter

150–175 g/5 1/2–6 oz caster sugar

4 green cardamom pods, bruised

4 cloves

2 x 1-cm/1/2-inch pieces cinnamon stick

300 ml/10 fl oz warm water

melted butter or vegetable oil, for brushing

55 g/2 oz seedless raisins

25 g/1 oz toasted flaked almonds, to decorate

single cream, to serve

The exotic perfume and delicious golden flesh of pineapple, combined with the seductive fragrance and the slender, silky grains of basmati rice bathed in the evocative richness of saffron – this is ambrosia in all its glory!

Preheat the oven to 160°C/325°F/Gas Mark 3. Soak the pounded saffron in the hot milk.

Wash the rice in several changes of cold water, then leave to drain in a colander.

Peel the pineapple and remove the 'eyes' with a small, sharp knife. Cut the flesh into bite-sized pieces.

Melt 1 tablespoon of the ghee in a large, heavy-based frying pan over a low heat. Add the pineapple, sprinkle with 2 tablespoons of the sugar and increase the heat to high. Cook, stirring, for 3–4 minutes, or until the pineapple begins to caramelize a little, then remove from the heat.

Melt the remaining ghee in a heavy-based saucepan over a low heat. Add the cardamom pods, cloves and cinnamon stick and cook, stirring, for 25–30 seconds. Add the rice, increase the heat slightly and cook, stirring, for 2–3 minutes. Add the saffron and milk and the warm water, bring to the boil and boil for 2 minutes, then reduce the heat to low. Cook, uncovered, for 2–3 minutes, until the surface liquid has been absorbed by the grains. Remove from the heat.

Brush the sides and the base of a lidded ovenproof dish with a little butter and add one-third of the rice. Top with one-third of the raisins, followed by one-third of the pineapple pieces. Sprinkle over one-third of the remaining sugar evenly. Repeat this process twice more, ensuring that you finish with a layer of raisins, pineapple and sugar.

Soak a piece of greaseproof paper, crumple it, then place loosely over the top layer of fruit and sugar. Cover with a piece of foil and seal the edges by pressing it round the entire rim. Put the lid on and bake in the centre of the preheated oven for 35–40 minutes. Turn off the oven and leave the rice to stand inside for 10–15 minutes.

Serve hot or cold, decorated with the flaked almonds and with cream to pour over.

# Ginger ice cream with date and tamarind sauce

## *Adrak, khajur aur imli ice cream*

**Serves 4-5**

*Ice cream*

1-litre/1³/4-pint carton vanilla ice cream

2 tsp ground ginger

*Tamarind sauce*

55 g/2 oz seedless raisins

85 g/3 oz stoned dried dates

250 ml/9 fl oz boiling water

2 rounded tsp tamarind concentrate or 3 tbsp tamarind juice

25 g/1 oz molasses sugar

200 g/7 oz chopped crystallized ginger, to serve

This is a cheat's version of a delicious and exotic Indian dessert, made with shop-bought vanilla ice cream blended with ground ginger and served with a tangy tamarind sauce. It provides the perfect way to round off a spicy meal.

Leave the ice cream at room temperature for 35–40 minutes to soften, then transfer to a bowl. Add the ground ginger and beat well. Return to the carton and freeze for 3–4 hours.

Meanwhile, to make the sauce, put the raisins and dates in a heatproof bowl, pour over the boiling water and leave to soak for 15–20 minutes. Transfer to a blender or food processor, add the tamarind and sugar and blend to a smooth purée. Transfer to a non-reactive bowl and leave to cool.

Put scoops of the ice cream into glasses and drizzle over the sauce. Arrange about 1 dessertspoon of crystallized ginger on top of each dessert and serve immediately. Serve any extra sauce separately.

# Thai

Thailand! Just the name sounds faraway and exotic, and the reality certainly lives up to the country's impressive reputation, with its vast array of fabulous buildings, a fascinating history, beautiful countryside and friendly people.

Thai food is an Asian cuisine and is famed for its vibrant, fresh taste and its delicate balance of flavours: hot, sour, sweet, salty and bitter. Bursting with variety, its dishes may be chilli hot, zesty with lime leaves or creamy with coconut.

# Appetizers

Starters should be tasty and small, just enough to whet the appetite before the main meal, and Thai cooking offers lots of ideal options. Many come perfectly packaged in parcels or wrappings of crisp pastry or omelette, others are handily sized in the form of little cakes or on skewers, and most are served with a flavourful sauce for dipping.

If you are entertaining on a relatively large scale, you can make a selection of these finger foods, rather like canapés, so that everyone can try a variety of different dishes. But if serving two to four people, a single recipe is easier to prepare and it will still satisfy your guests.

# Spicy Thai parcels

## *Kai yad sai talay*

**Serves 4**

**Omelettes**

4 eggs

2 tbsp water

3 spring onions, finely chopped

small handful of fresh coriander, finely chopped

groundnut or vegetable oil, for shallow-frying

soy sauce, to serve

**Filling**

1 tbsp groundnut or vegetable oil

3 spring onions, roughly chopped

225 g/8 oz raw squid, cleaned and cut into chunks if large or rings if small

115 g/4 oz raw prawns, peeled and deveined

115 g/4 oz skinned white fish fillet, such as cod or coley, cut into 2.5-cm/1-inch cubes

1 head pak choi, roughly chopped

1 tbsp green curry paste

1 tsp Thai fish sauce

You will need a good-quality non-stick 20-cm/8-inch frying pan to make these omelettes successfully, because they need to slide out easily onto a plate or chopping board.

Preheat the oven to 190°C/375°F/Gas Mark 5. For the omelettes, beat the eggs, water, spring onions and half the coriander together in a bowl. Heat 1 tablespoon of oil in a 20-cm/8-inch non-stick frying pan. Drizzle a quarter of the egg mixture over the base of the frying pan to make a rough lacy pattern. Cook over a medium–high heat for 2 minutes, or until just set, then use a palette knife to turn the omelette over and cook on the other side for 1 minute. Slide out onto a plate or chopping board. Repeat with the remaining mixture to make 3 more omelettes and add to the plate or board.

For the filling, heat the oil in the frying pan, add the spring onions and all the seafood and cook over a medium heat, stirring frequently, for 2–3 minutes, until the squid is firm, the prawns have turned pink and the fish is just cooked through. Transfer to a food processor and process for 30 seconds, or until just mixed. Add the pak choi, the remaining coriander, the curry paste and fish sauce and process again to a coarse mixture.

Arrange the omelettes on a chopping board and put a quarter of the seafood mixture in the centre of each. Roll one side of each omelette over the filling, fold in the adjacent 'sides' to cover the filling, then fold up the omelette to make a small, square parcel. Transfer the parcels to a baking sheet.

Bake in the preheated oven for 10–15 minutes, until lightly browned and cooked through. Serve immediately with soy sauce.

# Hot and sour soup

## *Tom yum*

**Serves 4**

2 fresh red chillies, deseeded
and roughly chopped

6 tbsp rice vinegar

1.2 litres/2 pints vegetable stock

2 lemon grass stalks, halved

4 tbsp soy sauce

1 tbsp palm sugar

juice of 1/2 lime

2 tbsp groundnut or vegetable oil

225 g/8 oz firm tofu
(drained weight), cut into
1-cm/1/2-inch cubes

400 g/14 oz canned straw
mushrooms, drained

4 spring onions, chopped

1 small head pak choi, shredded

This is a traditional, very popular Thai soup, with the heat provided by the chillies and sourness by the vinegar. Vary the balance of flavours according to your taste.

Mix the chillies and vinegar together in a non-reactive bowl, cover and leave to stand at room temperature for 1 hour.

Meanwhile, bring the stock to the boil in a saucepan. Add the lemon grass, soy sauce, sugar and lime juice, reduce the heat and simmer for 20–30 minutes.

Heat the oil in a preheated wok, add the tofu cubes and stir-fry over a high heat for 2–3 minutes, or until browned all over. (You may need to do this in 2 batches, depending on the size of the wok.) Remove with a slotted spoon and drain on kitchen paper.

Add the chillies and vinegar with the tofu, mushrooms and half the spring onions to the stock mixture and cook for 10 minutes. Mix the remaining spring onions with the pak choi and scatter over the soup before serving.

### Cook's tip
If you can't find canned straw mushrooms, use whole baby button mushrooms or quartered standard-sized button mushrooms instead.

# Crab, pork and chilli fritters

*Tod man moo sai boo*

**Serves 4**

*Fritters*

115 g/4 oz canned white crabmeat, drained

115 g/4 oz fresh pork mince

2 fresh red chillies, deseeded and roughly chopped

1 tsp salt

2 spring onions, chopped

handful of fresh coriander, chopped

1 egg white

groundnut or vegetable oil, for shallow-frying

*Dipping sauce*

150 ml/5 fl oz water

4 tbsp caster sugar

1 tbsp rice vinegar

1/2 small red onion, very finely diced

5-cm/2-inch piece cucumber, very finely diced

These delicious fritters can be made the day before and chilled in the refrigerator overnight to allow the flavours to develop. Serve on the day of cooking.

Put all the fritter ingredients except the oil in a food processor and process to a coarse paste. Use damp hands to shape into 20 small, flat cakes.

Heat enough oil to cover the base of a large frying pan, add the fritters, in 2–3 batches, and cook over a medium–high heat for 2 minutes on each side, or until browned and cooked through. Remove with a slotted spoon, drain on kitchen paper and keep warm while you cook the remaining fritters.

Meanwhile, to make the dipping sauce, put the water, sugar and vinegar in a small saucepan and heat gently until the sugar has dissolved. Add the onion and cucumber and simmer for 5 minutes. Serve warm, or cold, in a small serving dish with the fritters.

### Cook's tip

If you are making a large quantity of these fritters for a dinner party, cook them in several batches and transfer to a roasting tin. Warm them all up together in a hot oven until thoroughly heated through and serve immediately.

# Vegetable and black bean spring rolls

## *Por pia pak*

**Serves 4**

2 tbsp groundnut or vegetable oil, plus extra for deep-frying

4 spring onions, cut into 5-cm/ 2-inch lengths and shredded lengthways

2.5-cm/1-inch piece fresh ginger, peeled and finely chopped

1 large carrot, peeled and cut into matchsticks

1 red pepper, deseeded and cut into matchsticks

6 tbsp black bean sauce

55 g/2 oz fresh beansprouts

200 g/7 oz canned water chestnuts, drained and roughly chopped

5-cm/2-inch piece cucumber, cut into matchsticks

8 x 20-cm/8-inch square spring roll wrappers

sweet chilli dipping sauce, to serve (optional)

Spring rolls can be made with all sorts of fillings, so it's easy to adapt the ingredients as long as you keep the mixture fairly dry. Too much sauce and the pastry will become soggy.

Heat the oil in a preheated wok, add the spring onions, ginger, carrot and red pepper and stir-fry over a medium–high heat for 2–3 minutes. Add the black bean sauce, beansprouts, water chestnuts and cucumber and stir-fry for 1–2 minutes. Leave to cool.

Remove the spring roll wrappers from the packet, but keep them in a pile and covered with clingfilm to prevent them drying out. Lay one wrapper on a work surface in front of you in a diamond shape and brush the edges with water. Put a spoonful of the filling near one corner and fold the corner over the filling. Roll over again and then fold the side corners over the filling. Roll up to seal the filling completely. Repeat with the remaining wrappers and filling.

Heat enough oil for deep-frying in a wok, deep saucepan or deep-fat fryer to 180–190°C/ 350–375°F, or until a cube of bread browns in 30 seconds. Add the rolls, in 2–3 batches, and cook for 2–3 minutes until crisp and golden all over. Remove with a slotted spoon, drain on kitchen paper and keep warm while you cook the remaining rolls. Serve with sweet chilli dipping sauce, if using.

# Crispy pork dumplings

## *Kanom jeeb moo grob*

**Serves 4**

3 spring onions, roughly chopped

1 garlic clove, roughly chopped

1 small fresh red chilli, deseeded and roughly chopped

250 g/9 oz fresh pork mince

1 tsp salt

20 wonton wrappers

groundnut or vegetable oil, for deep-frying

**These dumplings can be steamed and then grilled if you prefer, but they are quicker to cook and crisper to eat when deep-fried.**

Put the spring onions, garlic, chilli, pork and salt in a food processor and process to a smooth paste.

Remove the wonton wrappers from the packet, but keep them in a pile and covered with clingfilm to prevent them drying out. Lay one wrapper on a work surface in front of you in a diamond shape and brush the edges with water. Put a small amount of filling near one edge and fold the wrapper over the filling. Press the edges together to seal the parcel and shape into a semicircle like a pasty. Repeat with the remaining wrappers and filling.

Heat enough oil for deep-frying in a wok, deep saucepan or deep-fat fryer to 180–190°C/350–375°F, or until a cube of bread browns in 30 seconds. Add the dumplings, in batches, and cook for 45 seconds–1 minute until crisp and golden all over. Remove with a slotted spoon, drain on kitchen paper and keep warm while you cook the remaining dumplings. Serve immediately once they are all cooked.

### Cook's tip

Always check the temperature of the oil before deep-frying. If the oil is smoking, it is too hot. Remove from the heat and leave to cool a little. Do not add too many dumplings at a time, otherwise the temperature of the oil will drop and this will make the dumplings soggy.

# Chicken satay skewers with peanut sauce

## *Satay gai*

**Serves 4**

4 skinless, boneless chicken breasts, about 115 g/4 oz each, cut into 2-cm/³/4-inch cubes

4 tbsp soy sauce

1 tbsp cornflour

2 garlic cloves, finely chopped

2.5-cm/1-inch piece fresh ginger, peeled and finely chopped

cucumber, roughly chopped, to serve

*Peanut sauce*

2 tbsp groundnut or vegetable oil

1/2 onion, finely chopped

1 garlic clove, finely chopped

4 tbsp crunchy peanut butter

4–5 tbsp water

1/2 tsp chilli powder

This is a simplified version of the ever-popular starter served in Thai restaurants. Marinating the chicken adds extra flavour.

Put the chicken cubes in a shallow dish. Mix the soy sauce, cornflour, garlic and ginger together in a small bowl and pour over the chicken. Cover and leave to marinate in the refrigerator for at least 2 hours. Meanwhile, soak 12 bamboo skewers in cold water for at least 30 minutes.

Preheat the oven to 190°C/375°F/Gas Mark 5. Divide the chicken cubes between the bamboo skewers. Heat a ridged griddle pan until hot, add the skewers and cook over a high heat for 3–4 minutes, turning occasionally, until browned all over. Transfer the skewers to a baking sheet and cook in the preheated oven for 5–8 minutes, until cooked through.

Meanwhile, to make the sauce, heat the oil in a saucepan, add the onion and garlic and cook over a medium heat, stirring frequently, for 3–4 minutes, until softened. Add the peanut butter, water and chilli powder and simmer for 2–3 minutes, until softened and thinned.

Serve the skewers immediately with the warm sauce and the cucumber.

## Cook's tip

Presoaking the bamboo skewers will help prevent them burning. You can also cut any excess length from the skewers if they are too long so that they fit within the griddle pan; this will stop the exposed ends burning.

# Prawn wraps

## *Gung gra borg*

**Serves 4**

24 cooked tail-on (peeled and tails left intact) king prawns

2 tbsp sweet chilli dipping sauce

24 wonton wrappers

groundnut or vegetable oil, for deep-frying

*Dipping sauce*

1 tbsp sesame oil

3 tbsp soy sauce

1-cm/½-inch piece fresh ginger, peeled and finely chopped

1 spring onion, finely chopped

Crisp pastry wrapped around succulent prawns makes a winning combination, and the dip adds heat and sweetness.

Toss the prawns in the chilli sauce in a bowl. Remove the wrappers from the packet, but keep them in a pile and covered with clingfilm to prevent them drying out. Lay one wrapper on a work surface in front of you and brush the edges with water. Place a prawn diagonally across the square and fold the wrapper around the prawn to enclose it completely, leaving the tail exposed. Repeat with the remaining wrappers and prawns.

Heat enough oil for deep-frying in a wok, deep saucepan or deep-fat fryer to 180–190°C/350–375°F, or until a cube of bread browns in 30 seconds. Add the wraps, in batches, and cook for 45 seconds–1 minute, until crisp and golden all over. Remove with a slotted spoon, drain on kitchen paper and keep warm while you cook the remaining wraps.

Meanwhile, to make the dipping sauce, mix the sesame oil, soy sauce, ginger and spring onion together in a bowl. Serve in small serving bowls with the wraps.

# Roasted sticky chicken wings

## *Peek gai ob*

**Serves 4**

12 chicken wings

3 tbsp tomato purée

3 tbsp soy sauce

1 tbsp palm sugar

2 tbsp sweet chilli dipping sauce

225 g/8 oz jasmine rice

2 tbsp rice vinegar

few fresh Thai basil leaves, chopped, plus extra whole leaves to garnish

groundnut or vegetable oil, for shallow-frying

It is always a particularly gratifying experience eating food with your fingers, and these sticky, sweet wings are a real treat. Make sure that you have plenty of serviettes and a finger bowl for guests.

Trim off the pointed tips of the wings, then arrange the wings in a roasting tin.

Mix the tomato purée, soy sauce, sugar and chilli sauce together in a small bowl and spoon over the chicken. Cover and leave to marinate in the refrigerator for 3 hours or overnight.

Meanwhile, cook the rice in a large saucepan of lightly salted boiling water for 12–15 minutes, or according to the packet instructions, until tender. Drain, return to the saucepan and stir in the vinegar and chopped basil.

Line a baking tin or shallow dish about 19 cm/7½ inches square with clingfilm. Press the rice into the tin or dish in an even layer about 2.5 cm/1 inch deep. Cover and leave to chill in the refrigerator while the chicken wings are marinating. Turn out of the tin, cut into 2.5-cm/1-inch cubes and set aside.

Preheat the oven to 200°C/400°F/Gas Mark 6. Roast the chicken wings in the preheated oven for 30–35 minutes until slightly blackened, sticky and tender and the juices run clear when a skewer is inserted into the thickest part of the meat.

Meanwhile, heat a little oil in a small saucepan or frying pan, add the whole basil leaves and cook over a medium–high heat, stirring, for a few seconds until crispy. Serve the chicken wings hot with the rice cubes, topped with the crispy basil leaves.

# Crab wontons

## *Kaiw phoo*

**Serves 4**

1 tbsp groundnut or vegetable oil, plus extra for deep-frying

2.5-cm/1-inch piece fresh ginger, peeled and finely chopped

1/4 red pepper, deseeded and finely chopped

handful of fresh coriander, chopped

1/4 tsp salt

150 g/5½ oz canned white crabmeat, drained

20 wonton wrappers

soy sauce or sweet chilli dipping sauce, to serve

The sweetness of the crabmeat combined with the crunch of the red pepper make these little parcels a tasty surprise to bite into.

Heat the oil in a preheated wok, add the ginger and red pepper and stir-fry over a high heat for 30 seconds. Add the coriander and mix well. Leave to cool, then add the salt and crabmeat and mix well.

Remove the wrappers from the packet, but keep them in a pile and covered with clingfilm to prevent them drying out. Lay one wrapper on a work surface in front of you and brush the edges with water. Put a teaspoonful of the crabmeat mixture in the centre and fold the wrapper over the mixture to form a triangle. Press the edges together to seal. Fold each side corner up to the top corner to make a small parcel, brushing the edges with water to seal if necessary. Repeat with the remaining wrappers and crabmeat mixture.

Heat enough oil for deep-frying in a wok, deep saucepan or deep-fat fryer to 180–190°C/ 350–375°F, or until a cube of bread browns in 30 seconds. Add the wontons, in batches, and cook for 45 seconds–1 minute, until crisp and golden all over. Remove with a slotted spoon, drain on kitchen paper and keep warm while you cook the remaining wontons. Serve with soy sauce or sweet chilli dipping sauce.

### Cook's tip

If fresh crabmeat is available, use instead of the canned crabmeat, but the latter is fine to use otherwise.

# Main Meals

Curries are obviously firm favourites when it comes to Thai main courses and the recipes featured include a classic Green Chicken Curry, together with that other great traditional dish, Masaman Curry with tender beef, peanuts and potatoes, as well as a sumptuous Mixed Fish and Coconut Curry. But there are other types of equally flavourful dishes, such as aromatic stir-fries and the irresistible Crispy Roast Duck – in this case served with wickedly fiery yet sweet pickled plums.

When cooking for a crowd, feel free to combine one of these recipes with a dish from the Rice and Noodles section, or serve with some of those invitingly crisp parcels from the Appetizers chapter.

# Green chicken curry

## *Gang kaiw wan gai*

**Serves 4**

2 tbsp groundnut or vegetable oil

4 spring onions, roughly chopped

2 tbsp green curry paste

700 ml/1¼ pints canned coconut milk

1 chicken stock cube

6 skinless, boneless chicken breasts, about 115 g/4 oz each, cut into 2.5-cm/1-inch cubes

large handful of fresh coriander, chopped

1 tsp salt

cooked rice or noodles, to serve

A very popular Thai dish that is easy to prepare and tastes fantastic. Poaching the chicken makes it very tender and the lime leaves add a tangy twist to the sauce.

Heat the oil in a preheated wok, add the spring onions and stir-fry over a medium–high heat for 30 seconds, or until starting to soften.

Add the curry paste, coconut milk and stock cube and bring gently to the boil, stirring occasionally. Add the chicken cubes, half the coriander and the salt and stir well. Reduce the heat and simmer gently for 8–10 minutes, until the chicken is cooked through and tender. Stir in the remaining coriander. Serve immediately with rice or noodles.

### Cook's tip
Use red curry paste if you like a hotter flavour. Other vegetables can be added and cooked in the coconut milk sauce.

# Spicy beef with black bean sauce

## *Nue pud tao jaiw*

The savoury taste of black bean sauce is wonderful with tender beef and shiitake mushrooms. Baby sweetcorn add extra flavour, texture and colour.

**Serves 2**

2 tbsp groundnut or vegetable oil

2 onions, cut into wedges

2 garlic cloves, finely chopped

1 tsp pepper

450 g/1 lb beef fillet, cut into thick strips

55 g/2 oz baby sweetcorn, halved lengthways

115 g/4 oz shiitake mushrooms, thickly sliced

6 tbsp soy sauce

125 g/4¹/₂ oz black bean sauce

1 tsp palm sugar

chopped fresh coriander, to garnish

cooked medium egg noodles, to serve

Heat the oil in a preheated wok, add the onions and stir-fry over a medium–high heat for 2–3 minutes, until starting to soften.

Add the garlic and pepper and stir well, then add the beef strips, baby sweetcorn and mushrooms and stir-fry over a high heat for 2–3 minutes. Add half the soy sauce, the black bean sauce and sugar and stir-fry for 1–2 minutes.

Serve immediately with egg noodles, tossed in the remaining soy sauce, garnished with chopped coriander.

## Cook's tip
This dish is equally tasty served with egg-fried rice or coriander rice.

# Chilli prawns with garlic noodles

## *Guay taiw phud gung*

**Serves 4**

200 g/7 oz cooked, peeled and deveined king or tiger prawns

4 tbsp sweet chilli dipping sauce

4 tbsp groundnut or vegetable oil

4 spring onions, chopped

55 g/2 oz mangetout, trimmed and halved diagonally

1 tbsp red curry paste

400 ml/14 fl oz canned coconut milk

55 g/2 oz canned, drained bamboo shoots

55 g/2 oz fresh beansprouts

*Garlic noodles*

115 g/4 oz dried medium egg noodles

2 garlic cloves, crushed

handful of fresh coriander, chopped

A hot and spicy dish for those chilli enthusiasts! The crunchy mangetout and beansprouts complement the hot flavours well.

Toss the prawns with the chilli sauce in a bowl. Cover and set aside.

Heat half the oil in a preheated wok, add the spring onions and mangetout and stir-fry over a medium–high heat for 2–3 minutes. Add the curry paste and stir well. Pour in the coconut milk and bring gently to the boil, stirring occasionally. Add the bamboo shoots and beansprouts and cook, stirring, for 1 minute. Stir in the prawns and chilli sauce, reduce the heat and simmer for 1–2 minutes, until just heated through.

Meanwhile, cook the noodles in a saucepan of lightly salted boiling water for 4–5 minutes, or according to the packet instructions, until just tender. Drain and return to the saucepan.

Heat the remaining oil in a small non-stick frying pan, add the garlic and stir-fry over a high heat for 30 seconds. Add to the drained noodles with half the coriander and toss together until well mixed.

Transfer the garlic noodles to 4 serving bowls, top with the chilli prawn mixture and serve immediately, garnished with the remaining coriander.

# Crispy roast duck with pickled plums

## *Ped grob gap plum dong*

The pickled plums may sound complicated, but they are easy to prepare and make an ideal accompaniment to other dishes, such as cold meats. But be warned – the pickled plums are chilli hot!

**Serves 4**

4 boneless duck breasts, about 175 g/6 oz each

3 spring onions, finely chopped

2 garlic cloves, finely chopped

4 tbsp oyster sauce

1 tbsp groundnut or vegetable oil

*To serve*

cooked noodles

stir-fried vegetables (optional)

*Pickled plums*

55 g/2 oz caster sugar

4 tbsp white wine vinegar

1 fresh red chilli, deseeded and finely chopped

1/2 tsp salt

4 plums, stoned and quartered

Use a sharp knife to make diagonal slashes in both directions in the skin of the duck breasts. Mix the spring onions, garlic and oyster sauce together in a small bowl and spread over the duck skin. Cover and leave to marinate in the refrigerator for 1 hour.

Meanwhile, to make the pickled plums, put all the ingredients except the plums in a saucepan and simmer gently for 10–15 minutes. Add the plums and simmer for a further 5 minutes, until just starting to soften. Leave to cool.

Preheat the oven to 200°C/400°F/Gas Mark 6. Heat the oil in a large frying pan, add the duck breasts, skin-side down, and cook for 2–3 minutes, until browned. Turn over and cook on the other side for 1–2 minutes.

Transfer the duck breasts to a roasting tin and roast in the preheated oven for 10–15 minutes, until just cooked through. Remove from the oven, cover with foil and leave to rest for 10 minutes.

Serve the duck breasts with the pickled plums, together with noodles and stir-fried vegetables, if using.

# Gingered chicken with cashew nuts and spring onions

*Gai phad met ma muang*

**Serves 4**

7.5-cm/3-inch piece fresh ginger, peeled and finely chopped

6 skinless, boneless chicken breasts, about 115 g/4 oz each, cut into 2.5-cm/1-inch cubes

2 tbsp sesame oil

4 tbsp groundnut or vegetable oil

1 onion, thinly sliced

2 garlic cloves, crushed

115 g/4 oz mushrooms, sliced

1 tsp salt

1/4 head Chinese leaves, roughly chopped

1 bunch spring onions, chopped

4 tbsp soy sauce

1 tsp Thai fish sauce

1 tsp palm sugar

50 g/1¾ oz unsalted cashew nuts

cooked rice or noodles, to serve (optional)

This simple yet flavourful dish makes an ideal packed lunch, as it tastes as good cold as it does when served hot.

Mix the ginger, chicken cubes and sesame oil together in a bowl. Cover and leave to marinate in the refrigerator for 2–3 hours.

Heat 3 tablespoons of the groundnut or vegetable oil in a preheated wok, add the onion and garlic and stir-fry over a medium–high heat for 2–3 minutes. Add the chicken mixture and stir-fry over a high heat for 2–3 minutes. Add the mushrooms, salt, Chinese leaves and half the spring onions and stir-fry for 3–4 minutes. Add the soy sauce, fish sauce and sugar and stir-fry for 2–3 minutes.

Meanwhile, heat the remaining groundnut or vegetable oil in a separate preheated wok or frying pan. Add the cashew nuts and the remaining spring onions and stir-fry over a high heat for 1 minute, or until the cashew nuts are golden and the spring onions are crispy. Scatter over the chicken mixture before serving with rice or noodles, if using.

# Minced pork kebabs with sweet chilli dipping sauce

*Moo kebab gab nam prik samrot*

**Serves 4**

1 large onion, chopped

2 garlic cloves, crushed

450 g/1 lb fresh pork mince

1 tsp salt

2 tbsp sweet chilli dipping sauce, plus extra to serve

handful of fresh coriander, chopped

1 egg

egg-fried rice, to serve

**These tasty kebabs make a great centrepiece for a dinner party when arranged across each other on a bed of rice, garnished with fresh coriander sprigs.**

Put all the ingredients except the rice in a food processor and process to a thick paste.

Divide the pork mixture into 8 portions. Using damp hands, squeeze one portion evenly around a flat metal skewer, then repeat to make 8 kebabs. Cover and chill in the refrigerator for at least 1 hour.

Cook the kebabs in a preheated ridged griddle pan over a medium–high heat or under a preheated medium–high grill, turning occasionally, for 5–6 minutes until browned all over and cooked through. Serve immediately on a bed of egg-fried rice with sweet chilli dipping sauce.

**Cook's tip**

Keep your hands damp with cold water to prevent the meat sticking to them as you form the pork mixture around the kebabs.

# Mixed fish and coconut curry

## *Gang talay*

Serves 4

2 tbsp groundnut or vegetable oil

6 spring onions, cut into 2.5-cm/
1-inch lengths

1 large carrot, peeled and cut
into matchsticks

55 g/2 oz green beans, trimmed
and cut into short lengths

2 tbsp red curry paste

700 ml/1¼ pints canned
coconut milk

225 g/8 oz skinned white fish fillet,
such as cod or coley, cut into
2.5-cm/1-inch cubes

225 g/8 oz squid, cleaned and cut
into thick rings

225 g/8 oz large raw prawns,
peeled and deveined

55 g/2 oz fresh beansprouts

115 g/4 oz dried rice noodles,
cooked according to the packet
instructions and drained

handful of fresh coriander, chopped

handful of fresh Thai basil leaves,
to garnish

Coconut and fish complement each other well, and this recipe really brings out the flavour of both. The Thai basil adds a wonderful freshness to this curry.

Heat the oil in a preheated wok, add the spring onions, carrot and green beans and stir-fry over a medium–high heat for 2–3 minutes, until starting to soften.

Stir in the curry paste, then add the coconut milk. Bring gently to the boil, stirring occasionally, then reduce the heat and simmer for 2–3 minutes. Add all the seafood and beansprouts and simmer for 2–3 minutes, until just cooked through and the prawns have turned pink.

Stir in the cooked noodles and coriander and cook for 1 minute. Serve immediately, scattered with the basil.

# Masaman curry

## *Gang masaman*

Serves 4

2 tbsp groundnut or vegetable oil

225 g/8 oz shallots, roughly chopped

1 garlic clove, crushed

450 g/1 lb beef fillet, thickly sliced and then cut into 2.5-cm/ 1-inch cubes

2 tbsp ready-made masaman curry paste

3 potatoes, peeled and cut into 2.5-cm/1-inch cubes

400 ml/14 fl oz canned coconut milk

2 tbsp soy sauce

150 ml/5 fl oz beef stock

1 tsp palm sugar

85 g/3 oz unsalted peanuts

handful of fresh coriander, chopped

cooked rice or noodles, to serve

A very traditional dish that combines potatoes and peanuts with tender beef fillet, and tastes fantastic!

Heat the oil in a preheated wok, add the shallots and garlic and stir-fry over a medium–high heat for 1–2 minutes, until softened. Add the beef cubes and curry paste and stir-fry over a high heat for 2–3 minutes, until browned all over. Add the potatoes, coconut milk, soy sauce, stock and sugar and bring gently to the boil, stirring occasionally. Reduce the heat and simmer for 8–10 minutes, until the potatoes are tender.

Meanwhile, heat a separate dry frying pan until hot, add the peanuts and cook over a medium–high heat, shaking the frying pan frequently, for 2–3 minutes, until lightly browned. Add to the curry with the coriander and stir well. Serve hot with rice or noodles.

### Cook's tip
To help the skins of the shallots come off more easily, put them in a heatproof bowl, cover with boiling water and leave for 10 minutes.

# Roast pork with pineapple

## *Moo ob saparot*

Serves 4

350 g/12 oz pork tenderloin

4 tbsp sweet chilli dipping sauce

4 tbsp soy sauce

1 tsp sugar

2 tbsp groundnut or vegetable oil

1 red onion, thinly sliced

1 carrot, peeled and cut into matchsticks

1 courgette, cut into matchsticks

115 g/4 oz canned water chestnuts, drained and sliced

2 fresh pineapple rings, peeled, cored and roughly chopped

cooked rice, to serve

The chilli flavour from the sauce and the sweetness from the pineapple make this a really fresh-tasting dish for summer evenings.

Put the pork in a shallow dish. Mix half the chilli sauce, the soy sauce and sugar together in a small bowl and brush over the pork. Cover and leave to marinate in the refrigerator overnight.

Preheat the oven to 200°C/400°F/Gas Mark 6. Heat a ridged griddle pan or frying pan until hot, add the pork and cook over a high heat for 1 minute on each side, or until browned. Transfer to a roasting tin and roast in the preheated oven for 15–20 minutes, until cooked through. Thinly slice the pork, then cut each slice into strips.

Heat the oil in a preheated wok, add the onion, carrot and courgette and stir-fry over a medium–high heat for 2–3 minutes. Add the water chestnuts, the remaining chilli sauce and the chopped pineapple rings and stir-fry for 1 minute. Add the pork and stir-fry for 1 minute. Serve immediately with rice.

### Cook's tip
You can use canned pineapple, drained, instead of fresh in this dish.

# Vegetarian

Thai food offers vegetarians a tasty, healthy and flexible approach to cooking and is bursting with fragrant and fiery flavours as well as colour and texture. Tofu, or soya bean curd, provides an excellent source of vegetable protein and can easily be infused with flavour by marinating. Unsalted cashew nuts or peanuts are also highly nutritious and contribute an extra crunchiness to stir-fries and other Thai dishes.

Although the vegetables used can vary according to what is available and seasonal, some are used specifically for their particular qualities in the curry dishes, such as potato teamed with spinach.

# Cauliflower, broccoli and cashew nut salad

## Yum dokralam metmamuang

**Serves 4**

2 tbsp groundnut or vegetable oil

2 red onions, cut into wedges

1 small head cauliflower, cut into florets

1 small head broccoli, cut into florets

2 tbsp ready-made yellow curry paste or red curry paste

400 ml/14 fl oz canned coconut milk

1 tsp Thai fish sauce

1 tsp palm sugar

1 tsp salt

85 g/3 oz unsalted cashew nuts

handful of fresh coriander, chopped, plus extra sprigs, torn, to garnish

**This main dish is full of vitamins. Keep it crunchy by cooking the vegetables for a short length of time and adding the nuts at the last minute.**

Heat the oil in a preheated wok, add the onions and stir-fry over a medium–high heat for 3–4 minutes, until starting to brown. Add the cauliflower and broccoli and stir-fry for 1–2 minutes. Stir in the curry paste and stir-fry for 30 seconds, then add the coconut milk, fish sauce, sugar and salt. Bring gently to the boil, stirring occasionally, then reduce the heat and simmer gently for 3–4 minutes, until the vegetables are almost tender.

Meanwhile, heat a separate dry frying pan until hot, add the cashew nuts and cook, shaking the frying pan frequently, for 2–3 minutes, until lightly browned. Add to the stir-fry with the coriander, stir well and serve immediately, garnished with torn sprigs of coriander.

# Mixed mushrooms with spinach and beansprouts

## *Pat puk ruamit*

**Serves 4**

2 tbsp groundnut or vegetable oil

1 bunch spring onions, roughly chopped

1 garlic clove, crushed

2.5-cm/1-inch piece fresh ginger, peeled and finely chopped

175 g/6 oz shiitake mushrooms, halved

175 g/6 oz closed-cup mushrooms, quartered

175 g/6 oz baby button mushrooms

3 tbsp soy sauce

115 g/4 oz spinach leaves

55 g/2 oz fresh beansprouts

2 tbsp sweet chilli dipping sauce

noodles or cooked rice, to serve

**Various different kinds of mushroom are now widely available, so try different combinations in this recipe for flavour and texture variation.**

Heat the oil in a preheated wok, add the spring onions and stir-fry over a medium–high heat for 1–2 minutes. Add the garlic and ginger and stir-fry for 1–2 minutes. Add all the mushrooms and stir-fry over a high heat for 2–3 minutes, until starting to soften and brown.

Add the soy sauce, spinach and beansprouts and stir-fry for 2–3 minutes, until the spinach has wilted. Stir in the chilli sauce. Serve immediately with noodles or rice.

## Cook's tip

It is more economical to use spinach that you have to wash yourself, but if in a hurry, use the ready-washed variety.

# Crispy vegetable stir-fry salad

## *Yum puk grob*

**Serves 4**

2 tbsp groundnut or vegetable oil

1 bunch spring onions,
roughly chopped

2.5-cm/1-inch piece fresh ginger,
peeled and finely chopped

2 lemon grass stalks, halved

2 carrots, peeled and cut into
matchsticks

1 small head broccoli, cut into
florets

55 g/2 oz baby sweetcorn,
halved lengthways

55 g/2 oz canned water chestnuts,
drained

1 tbsp red curry paste

225 g/8 oz dried medium
egg noodles

4 tbsp sesame seeds

You can use any mix of vegetables for this stir-fry, according to what is available and looks appealing or what is on special offer on the day.

Heat the oil in a preheated wok, add the spring onions, ginger and lemon grass and stir-fry over a medium–high heat for 2–3 minutes, until starting to soften. Add the carrots, broccoli and baby sweetcorn and stir-fry for 3–4 minutes, until starting to soften. Add the water chestnuts and curry paste and stir well, then stir-fry for a further 2–3 minutes. Discard the lemon grass.

Meanwhile, cook the noodles in a large saucepan of lightly salted boiling water for 4–5 minutes, or according to the packet instructions, until just tender. Drain and return to the saucepan. Add the sesame seeds and toss to coat.

Add the noodles to the stir-fried vegetables and serve immediately.

### Cook's tip
Cut all the vegetables to a similiar size so that they cook in the same length of time.

# Chunky potato and spinach curry

## *Gang puk*

**Serves 4**

4 tomatoes

2 tbsp groundnut or vegetable oil

2 onions, cut into thick wedges

2.5-cm/1-inch piece fresh ginger, peeled and finely chopped

1 garlic clove, chopped

2 tbsp ground coriander

450 g/1 lb peeled potatoes, cut into chunks

600 ml/1 pint vegetable stock

1 tbsp red curry paste

225 g/8 oz spinach leaves

cooked rice or noodles, to serve (optional)

Potatoes in curry are always delicious, but become sublime when mixed with spinach. A favourite combination in Indian curries, it works equally well in Thai cooking.

Put the tomatoes in a heatproof bowl and cover with boiling water. Leave for 2–3 minutes, then plunge into cold water and peel off the skins. Cut each tomato into quarters and remove and discard the seeds and central core. Set aside.

Heat the oil in a preheated wok, add the onions, ginger and garlic and stir-fry over a medium–high heat for 2–3 minutes, until starting to soften. Add the coriander and potatoes and stir-fry for 2–3 minutes. Add the stock and curry paste and bring to the boil, stirring occasionally. Reduce the heat and simmer gently for 10–15 minutes, until the potatoes are tender.

Add the spinach and the tomato quarters and cook, stirring, for 1 minute, or until the spinach has wilted. Serve with rice or noodles, if using.

# Peanut tofu skewers

## *Tofu tua barbecue*

Tofu absorbs marinades well, which gives it more flavour, since otherwise it can be rather bland. It is also firm enough to remain on the skewers if cooked quickly.

**Serves 4**

225 g/8 oz firm tofu (drained weight), cut into 2.5-cm/1-inch cubes

1 tbsp groundnut or vegetable oil

5 tbsp soy sauce

1 fresh red chilli, deseeded and sliced

1 garlic clove, crushed

2 tbsp crunchy peanut butter

2 red peppers, deseeded and cut into 2.5-cm/1-inch squares

1 courgette, cut into thick slices

175 g/6 oz dried rice noodles

3 tbsp sweet chilli dipping sauce

1/2 cucumber, chopped

55 g/2 oz unsalted peanuts, chopped

handful of fresh coriander, chopped, to garnish

Pat the tofu cubes dry with kitchen paper. Put the oil, soy sauce, chilli, garlic and peanut butter in a food processor and process to a paste. Transfer to a bowl and stir the tofu cubes into the marinade. Cover and leave to marinate in the refrigerator for 1 hour. Meanwhile, soak 8 bamboo skewers in cold water.

Thread the tofu cubes, red pepper squares and courgette slices alternately onto the skewers and brush with any remaining marinade. Cook in a preheated ridged griddle pan over a medium–high heat or under a preheated medium–high grill, turning occasionally, for 3–4 minutes, until browned all over.

Meanwhile, soak the noodles in a saucepan of boiling water, covered, for 4 minutes, or according to the packet instructions.

Drain the noodles and transfer to a bowl. Add the chilli sauce, cucumber and peanuts and toss to coat. Divide between 4 servings plates and top with 2 skewers each. Serve immediately, garnished with the coriander.

# Butternut squash curry

## Gang butternut

**Serves 4**

2 tbsp groundnut or vegetable oil

1 tsp cumin seeds

2 red onions, sliced

2 celery sticks, sliced

1 large butternut squash, peeled, deseeded and cut into chunks

2 tbsp green curry paste

300 ml/10 fl oz vegetable stock

2 fresh kaffir lime leaves

55 g/2 oz fresh beansprouts

handful of fresh coriander, chopped, to garnish

cooked rice, to serve

The bright orange of the squash and the green of the celery make this a colourful dish to serve. The lime leaves add an intense citrus flavour.

Heat the oil in a preheated wok, add the cumin seeds and stir-fry over a medium–high heat for 2–3 minutes, until starting to pop. Add the onions and celery and stir-fry for 2–3 minutes. Add the squash and stir-fry for 3–4 minutes. Add the curry paste, stock and lime leaves and bring to the boil, stirring occasionally.

Reduce the heat and simmer gently for 3–4 minutes, until the squash is tender. Add the beansprouts and cook for a further 1–2 minutes, until hot but still crunchy. Scatter the coriander over the curry and serve immediately with rice.

### Cook's tip
It is easier to peel the squash if you cut it into pieces first, as it is very hard. Use a small, sharp knife rather than a vegetable peeler.

# Aubergine curry

## *Gang makua*

**Serves 2**

groundnut or vegetable oil,
for deep-frying, plus 2 tbsp

2 aubergines, cut into 2-cm/3/4-inch
cubes

1 bunch spring onions,
roughly chopped

2 garlic cloves, chopped

2 red peppers, deseeded and
cut into 2-cm/3/4-inch squares

3 courgettes, thickly sliced

400 ml/14 fl oz canned
coconut milk

2 tbsp red curry paste

large handful of fresh coriander,
chopped, plus extra leaves
to garnish

cooked rice or noodles, to serve

The combination of aubergines, peppers and courgettes in this recipe, inspired by the classic French dish ratatouille, works equally successfully in this delicious curry.

Heat enough oil for deep-frying in a wok, deep saucepan or deep-fat fryer to 180–190°C/350–375°F, or until a cube of bread browns in 30 seconds. Add the aubergine cubes, in batches, and cook for 45 seconds–1 minute, until crisp and brown all over. Remove with a slotted spoon and drain on kitchen paper.

Heat the remaining 2 tablespoons of oil in a separate preheated wok or large frying pan, add the spring onions and garlic and stir-fry over a medium–high heat for 1 minute. Add the red peppers and courgettes and stir-fry for 2–3 minutes. Add the coconut milk and curry paste and bring gently to the boil, stirring occasionally. Add the aubergines and coriander, reduce the heat and simmer for 2–3 minutes.

Serve immediately with rice or noodles, garnished with coriander leaves.

# Sweet and sour salad

## Yum puk ruam mit

**Serves 4**

1/4 cucumber, peeled, halved, deseeded and sliced

55 g/2 oz fresh beansprouts

1 large carrot, peeled and cut into matchsticks

1 red pepper, deseeded and sliced

4–5 Chinese leaves, shredded

1 mango, stoned, peeled and sliced

few fresh Thai basil leaves, torn into pieces

*Dressing*

5 tbsp groundnut oil

5 spring onions, chopped

2 tbsp rice vinegar

1 tbsp caster sugar

1 small fresh red chilli, deseeded and finely chopped

2 tbsp pineapple juice

A colourful and surprising mixture of fruit and vegetables that makes a refreshing light lunch or starter on warm, sunny days.

Put all the dressing ingredients in a saucepan and bring gently to the boil. Reduce the heat and simmer for 3–4 minutes, until the spring onions are softened. Leave to cool.

Put all the prepared salad ingredients in a large bowl. Pour the dressing over, add the basil and toss to coat.

### Cook's tip

Use a teaspoon to scoop the seeds out of the cucumber. To prepare the mango, cut lengthways either side of the flat central stone. Discard this central slice. Peel the remaining pieces of fruit and slice.

# Red curry with mixed leaves

## *Gang dang puk*

**Serves 4**

2 tbsp groundnut or vegetable oil

2 onions, thinly sliced

1 bunch fine asparagus spears

400 ml/14 fl oz canned coconut milk

2 tbsp red curry paste

3 fresh kaffir lime leaves

225 g/8 oz baby spinach leaves

2 heads pak choi, chopped

1 small head Chinese leaves, shredded

handful of fresh coriander, chopped

cooked rice, to serve

**This eye-catching mixture of green shoots and leaves should be cooked quickly to retain the varied textures of the ingredients.**

Heat the oil in a preheated wok, add the onions and asparagus and stir-fry over a medium–high heat for 1–2 minutes.

Add the coconut milk, curry paste and lime leaves and bring gently to the boil, stirring occasionally. Add the spinach, pak choi and Chinese leaves and cook, stirring, for 2–3 minutes, until wilted. Add the coriander and stir well. Serve immediately with rice.

### Cook's tip
For non-vegetarians, scatter some shredded or diced cooked chicken or cooked peeled prawns over the cooked rice to accompany the curry.

# Rice and Noodles

We usually think of rice and noodles as accompaniments to main dishes, but they can make an equally satisfying lunch or supper in their own right. In Thai cooking, flavour is incorporated into plain rice by first stir-frying it in oil and then cooking it in stock and/or coconut milk.

Egg noodles and rice noodles offer a contrast in both texture and taste, and they also come in different thicknesses. Where noodles form a main part of the dish, they first need to be cooked in boiling water. To prevent them sticking together after draining, rinse under cold running water ready to use later or toss them in groundnut or vegetable oil or soy sauce. They are usually added to the other ingredients at the final stage.

# Pad Thai

## *Pad thai*

**Serves 4**

225 g/8 oz thick dried rice noodles

2 tbsp groundnut or vegetable oil

4 spring onions, roughly chopped

2 garlic cloves, crushed

2 fresh red chillies, deseeded
and sliced

225 g/8 oz pork fillet, trimmed and
thinly sliced

115 g/4 oz cooked peeled
large prawns

juice of 1 lime

2 tbsp Thai fish sauce

2 eggs, beaten

55 g/2 oz fresh beansprouts

handful of fresh coriander, chopped

55 g/2 oz unsalted peanuts,
chopped

This traditional Thai dish has many variations, but should always include noodles and peanuts. It is important to use thick rice noodles, which are now widely available.

Soak the noodles in a large saucepan of boiling water, covered, for 10 minutes, or according to the packet instructions, until just tender. Drain, rinse under cold running water and set aside.

Heat the oil in a preheated wok, add the spring onions, garlic and chillies and stir-fry over a medium–high heat for 1–2 minutes. Add the pork and stir-fry over a high heat for 1–2 minutes, until browned all over.

Add the prawns, lime juice, fish sauce and eggs and stir-fry over a medium heat for 2–3 minutes, until the eggs have set and the prawns are heated through.

Add the beansprouts, most of the coriander, the peanuts and the noodles and stir-fry for 30 seconds, until heated through. Serve immediately, garnished with the remaining coriander.

# Egg-fried rice with prawns and peppers

*Cow phat gung sai kai*

**Serves 4**

*Egg-fried rice*

225 g/8 oz jasmine rice

1 tbsp groundnut or vegetable oil

2 spring onions, finely chopped

2 eggs, beaten

handful of fresh coriander, chopped, plus extra sprigs to garnish

*Prawns and peppers*

55 g/2 oz creamed coconut

150 ml/5 fl oz boiling water

4 tbsp groundnut or vegetable oil

2 fresh red chillies, deseeded and roughly chopped

6 spring onions, roughly chopped

350 g/12 oz cooked peeled prawns

juice of 1/2 lemon

6 fresh Thai basil leaves, torn

1 tbsp Thai fish sauce

1 red pepper, deseeded and cut into strips

Pink prawns and red peppers cooked with creamed coconut add an exciting, colourful dimension to this well-loved rice dish.

Cook the rice in a large saucepan of lightly salted boiling water for 12–15 minutes, or according to the packet instructions, until just tender. Rinse under cold running water, fluff up with a fork and leave to cool completely.

Heat the oil in a preheated wok, add the spring onions and stir-fry over a medium–high heat for 30 seconds. Add the rice and stir-fry for 1–2 minutes, or until heated through. Push all the rice to one side of the wok and tilt the pan to allow any oil to run to the opposite side. While still tilted, add the eggs and cook over a medium heat, stirring constantly, for 2–3 minutes, until set. Return the wok to a level position, add the coriander and stir the rice through the cooked eggs. Remove from the heat but keep the rice warm in the wok.

For the prawns and peppers, chop the creamed coconut and dissolve in the boiling water. Heat half the oil in a separate preheated wok or large frying pan, add the chillies and spring onions and stir-fry over a medium–high heat for 1–2 minutes, until just tender. Add the prawns, coconut mixture, lemon juice, basil and fish sauce and bring gently to the boil, stirring occasionally, to ensure that the prawns are heated through.

Heat the remaining oil in a small frying pan, add the red pepper and stir-fry over a high heat for 1–2 minutes, until sizzling and lightly browned. Stir into the prawn mixture and serve immediately with the egg-fried rice and garnished with sprigs of coriander.

## Cook's tip

Base-line 4 ramekin dishes with baking paper and divide the rice between them. Press down and then turn out the rice to serve as timbales.

# Red roasted pork with peppered noodles

*Chad guay taiw moo dang*

**Serves 2**

1 tbsp red curry paste

2 tbsp soy sauce

350 g/12 oz piece pork fillet, trimmed

225 g/8 oz fine dried egg noodles

2 tbsp groundnut or vegetable oil

1 red onion, chopped

2.5-cm/1-inch piece fresh ginger, peeled and finely chopped

1 garlic clove, finely chopped

1 orange pepper, deseeded and chopped

1 red pepper, deseeded and chopped

1 tbsp black pepper

1 small bunch fresh chives, snipped

handful of fresh coriander, chopped

Red curry paste provides a hot and spicy coating for tender pork fillet, which is then sliced and served on top of an egg noodle stir-fry enlivened with both sweet peppers and hot black pepper.

Mix the curry paste and soy sauce together in a small bowl and spread over the pork fillet. Cover and leave to marinate in the refrigerator for 1 hour.

Preheat the oven to 200°C/400°F/Gas Mark 6. Roast the pork in the preheated oven for 20–25 minutes, until cooked through. Remove from the oven, cover with foil and leave to rest for 15 minutes.

Meanwhile, cook the noodles in a large saucepan of boiling water for 4 minutes, or according to the packet instructions, until just tender. Drain, rinse under cold running water and set aside.

Heat the oil in a preheated wok, add the onion, ginger and garlic and stir-fry over a medium–high heat for 1–2 minutes. Add the orange and red peppers and pepper and stir-fry for 2–3 minutes, until tender. Stir in the chives and most of the coriander.

Add the drained noodles to the pepper mixture and toss together until well mixed. Divide between 2 serving dishes. Slice the pork and arrange on top of the noodles. Scatter with the remaining coriander and serve immediately.

# Thai fish cakes with coconut rice

## *Tod man pla gap cow krati*

**Serves 4**

*Fish cakes*

450 g/1 lb skinned white fish fillets, such as cod or coley, roughly cut into chunks

6 spring onions, finely chopped

1–2 tbsp red curry paste

1 tbsp Thai fish sauce

2 egg whites

groundnut or vegetable oil, for shallow-frying

*Coconut rice*

2 tbsp groundnut or vegetable oil

1 onion, chopped

225 g/8 oz jasmine rice

400 ml/14 fl oz canned coconut milk

1 tbsp red curry paste

1 tbsp Thai fish sauce

handful of fresh coriander, chopped

*To serve*

lime wedges

sweet chilli dipping sauce (optional)

It's quick and easy to whiz up the fish cake mixture, but you need time to pat them into shape and cook them. You can serve them on their own with a sweet chilli dipping sauce as a starter.

For the fish cakes, put all the ingredients except the oil in a food processor and process to a coarse paste. Use damp hands to shape into 12 small, flat cakes. Cover and chill in the refrigerator for 30 minutes.

For the coconut rice, heat the oil in a preheated wok, add the onion and stir-fry over a medium–high heat for 2 minutes. Add the rice and stir-fry for 30 seconds, until coated with the oil. Add the coconut milk, curry paste and fish sauce and bring gently to the boil, stirring occasionally. Reduce the heat and simmer gently for 10–15 minutes, until the rice is tender, adding a little boiling water or stock if necessary. Stir in the coriander.

Meanwhile, heat enough oil to cover the base of a large frying pan, add the fish cakes, in batches, and cook over a medium heat for 3 minutes, then turn over and cook on the other side for 2 minutes, or until browned on both sides. Remove with a slotted spoon, drain on kitchen paper and keep warm while you cook the remaining fish cakes.

Spoon the rice onto serving plates, top with a few fish cakes and serve with lime wedges and sweet chilli dipping sauce, if using.

# Chilli rice with stir-fried beef

## *Cow phad nue prik*

Thickly sliced beef fillet can take a strong savoury flavour and makes a great combination when served with hot chilli rice. A good red wine would be ideal served with this meal.

**Serves 4**

*Chilli rice*

2 tbsp groundnut or vegetable oil

5 spring onions, chopped

55 g/2 oz fine green beans, trimmed and halved

2 fresh red chillies, deseeded and sliced

225 g/8 oz basmati rice

600 ml/1 pint beef stock

*Stir-fried beef*

2 tbsp groundnut or vegetable oil

1 onion, cut into wedges

1 green pepper, deseeded and cut into chunks

2.5-cm/1-inch piece fresh ginger, peeled and finely chopped

350 g/12 oz beef fillet, cut into strips

6 tbsp oyster sauce

2 tbsp soy sauce

1 tsp palm sugar

handful of fresh coriander, chopped

To make the chilli rice, heat the oil in a preheated wok, add the spring onions, green beans and chillies and stir-fry over a medium–high heat for 1–2 minutes. Add the rice and stir-fry for 2–3 minutes. Add the stock and bring to the boil, stirring occasionally. Reduce the heat and simmer gently for 10–15 minutes, until the rice is tender, adding more stock if necessary. Remove from the heat but keep the rice warm in the wok.

To make the stir-fried beef, heat the oil in a separate preheated wok or large frying pan, add the onion, green pepper and ginger and stir-fry over a medium–high heat for 30 seconds. Add the beef and stir-fry over a high heat for 1–2 minutes, until browned all over. Add the oyster sauce, soy sauce and sugar and stir-fry for 2–3 minutes, until heated through. Serve immediately with the chilli rice, scattered with the coriander.

### Cook's tip

To give the stir-fry extra crunch and colour, halve baby sweetcorn and add to the wok or frying pan with the onion, green pepper and ginger.

# Squid and prawn laksa

## *Tom ka talay*

**Serves 4**

- 225 g/8 oz dried rice noodles
- 700 ml/1¼ pints canned coconut milk
- 2 fish stock cubes
- 3 fresh kaffir lime leaves
- 2 tbsp red curry paste
- 1 bunch spring onions, roughly chopped
- 2 fresh red chillies, deseeded and roughly chopped
- 225 g/8 oz raw squid, cleaned and cut into rings
- 225 g/8 oz large raw prawns, peeled and deveined
- handful of fresh coriander, chopped, plus leaves to garnish

Most fishmongers and supermarkets sell squid ready cleaned so that you don't have to prepare it yourself. It usually comes frozen, so you will need to thaw it in the refrigerator before using.

Soak the noodles in a saucepan of boiling water for 4 minutes, covered, until just tender, or according to the packet instructions. Drain, rinse under cold running water and set aside.

Put the coconut milk, stock cubes, lime leaves, curry paste, spring onions and chillies in a large saucepan and bring gently to the boil, stirring occasionally. Reduce the heat and simmer, stirring occasionally, for 2–3 minutes, until the stock cubes and paste have dissolved. Add the squid and prawns and simmer for 1–2 minutes, until the squid has plumped up and the prawns have turned pink. Add the cooked noodles and coriander and stir well. Serve immediately in soup bowls, garnished with coriander leaves.

### Cook's tip

Fresh kaffir lime leaves can be kept in a freezer bag in the freezer. Take out as many as you need at the time. Dried lime leaves are also available in packs, but the fresh ones add much more flavour.

# Chicken curry with fried noodles

## Gang gai mee grob

**Serves 4**

2 tbsp groundnut or vegetable oil, plus extra for deep-frying

4 skinless, boneless chicken breasts, about 115 g/4 oz each, cut into 2.5-cm/1-inch cubes

2 red onions, roughly chopped

5 spring onions, roughly chopped

2 garlic cloves, finely chopped

1 fresh green chilli, deseeded and finely chopped

175 g/6 oz shiitake mushrooms, thickly sliced

2 tbsp green curry paste

400 ml/14 fl oz canned coconut milk

300 ml/10 fl oz chicken stock

2 fresh kaffir lime leaves

handful of fresh coriander, chopped

handful of fresh chives, snipped

25 g/1 oz dried thin rice noodles

cooked rice, to serve (optional)

The rice noodles puff up really quickly in hot oil – great entertainment for children to watch at a safe distance – but take care as they are done in a matter of seconds.

Heat the oil in a preheated wok, add the chicken cubes, in batches, and stir-fry over a medium–high heat for 3–4 minutes, until lightly browned all over. Remove with a slotted spoon, transfer to a plate and set aside.

Add the red onions and spring onions, garlic and chilli to the wok and stir-fry over a medium heat, adding a little more oil if necessary, for 2–3 minutes, until softened but not browned. Add the mushrooms and stir-fry over a high heat for 30 seconds. Return the chicken to the wok.

Add the curry paste, coconut milk, stock and lime leaves and bring gently to the boil, stirring occasionally. Reduce the heat and simmer gently for 4–5 minutes, until the chicken is tender and cooked through. Stir in the coriander and chives.

Meanwhile, heat enough oil for deep-frying in a separate wok, a deep saucepan or deep-fat fryer to 180–190°C/350–375°F, or until a cube of bread browns in 30 seconds. Divide the noodles into 4 portions and cook, one portion at a time, for about 2 seconds until puffed up and crisp. Remove with a slotted spoon and drain on kitchen paper.

Serve the curry with rice, if using, topped with the crispy noodles.

# Spicy chicken kebabs with coriander rice

## Gai kebab gao cow

Serves 4

*Chicken kebabs*

3 tbsp oyster sauce

2 tbsp soy sauce, plus extra
for serving

2.5-cm/1-inch piece fresh ginger,
peeled and finely chopped

4 tbsp honey

2 tsp soft dark brown sugar

2 tsp cornflour

4 skinless, boneless chicken
breasts, about 115 g/4 oz each,
cut into 2.5-cm/1-inch cubes

2 red peppers, deseeded and cut
into 2.5-cm/1-inch squares

*Coriander rice*

2 tbsp groundnut or vegetable oil

6 spring onions, chopped

225 g/8 oz jasmine rice

600 ml/1 pint chicken stock

115 g/4 oz pak choi,
roughly chopped

115 g/4 oz baby spinach leaves

large handful of fresh coriander,
chopped

The honey adds sweetness and stickiness to the chicken. Cook over a high heat to char the chicken before finishing off in the oven.

Soak 8 bamboo skewers in cold water for at least 30 minutes. For the kebabs, mix all the ingredients except the chicken cubes and red peppers together in a bowl. Add the chicken cubes and toss to coat. Cover and leave to marinate in the refrigerator for 2 hours.

Preheat the oven to 190°C/375°F/Gas Mark 5. Divide the chicken cubes and red pepper squares between the skewers, threading them alternately onto the skewers. Heat a ridged griddle pan until hot, add the skewers and cook over a high heat for 3–4 minutes, turning occasionally, until browned all over. Transfer to a baking sheet and cook in the preheated oven for a further 10–12 minutes, until cooked through.

Meanwhile, to make the coriander rice, heat the oil in a preheated wok, add the spring onions and stir-fry over a medium–high heat for 30 seconds, or until softened. Add the rice and stir-fry for 2–3 minutes. Add the stock and bring to the boil, stirring occasionally. Reduce the heat and simmer for 10–12 minutes, until the rice is tender, adding more stock or boiling water if necessary. Add the pak choi, spinach and coriander and cook, stirring, for 1–2 minutes, until wilted.

Spoon the rice onto serving plates, top with the chicken kebabs and a little extra soy sauce and serve immediately.

# Spring vegetable rice

## Khao pat puk

Serves 4

2 tbsp groundnut or vegetable oil

2 shallots, chopped

2 garlic cloves, crushed

225 g/8 oz basmati rice

600 ml/1 pint chicken stock

1 tbsp red curry paste

1 tsp Thai fish sauce

3 tbsp soy sauce

175 g/6 oz baby sweetcorn, halved lengthways

115 g/4 oz baby carrots, halved lengthways

55 g/2 oz sugar snap peas

55 g/2 oz fresh beansprouts

4 tbsp sesame seeds

handful of fresh coriander, chopped

2 tbsp sesame oil

An ideal quick and easy supper after the long winter, when all the baby spring vegetables come onto the supermarket shelves. You can also add asparagus spears to the medley when available.

Heat the oil in a preheated wok, add the shallots and garlic and stir-fry over a medium–high heat for 1–2 minutes. Add the rice and stir-fry for 2–3 minutes. Add the stock, curry paste, fish sauce and soy sauce and bring to the boil, stirring occasionally. Reduce the heat and simmer for 10–12 minutes, until the rice is tender, adding more stock or boiling water, if necessary,

Meanwhile, cook the baby sweetcorn and carrots in a saucepan of lightly salted boiling water for 2–3 minutes, until just tender. Add the sugar snap peas and cook for 1 minute. Add the beansprouts, stir well, then drain.

Heat a dry frying pan until hot, add the sesame seeds and cook over a medium–high heat, shaking the frying pan frequently, for 30–45 seconds, until lightly browned.

Add the drained vegetables, coriander and sesame oil to the rice and serve immediately, scattered with the toasted sesame seeds.

# Vietnamese

Vietnam sits at South East Asia's eastern edge, a cultural crossroads, and its civilization has been forged through millennia of conflict and migration.

Vietnam's turbulent history has resulted in a cuisine that is an incredible fusion of influences from China, South Asia, France and, to a lesser extent, North America. Vietnamese cuisine is like no other in the world – it is at once familiar and unexpected, yet always fresh and exciting.

# Soups, Rice
# and Noodles

Rice forms part of nearly every Vietnamese meal, not only in rice dishes but rice-based noodles, often added to soups, rolls and crêpes, which feature here in this collection of simple-to-prepare, flavourful dishes.

Recipes include Rice Noodle Soup with Beef: the famous Northern soup, where slices of tender steak are cooked in steaming stock; and fragrant, palate-cleansing clear soups, as well as crisp-coated chunks of fish served over noodles. There are also some real showstoppers: lacy Vietnamese crêpes make an elegant meal in themselves, while spring and summer rolls deliver restaurant flair at home, and Beef Fondue is the perfect dish for relaxed entertaining.

# Spicy and sour fish and pineapple soup

## Canh ca nau dua

**Serves 6**

450 g/1 lb skinless, boneless cod fillets, cut into large chunks

100 ml/3½ fl oz tamarind concentrate

225 g/8 oz peeled and cored ripe pineapple, cut into bite-sized chunks

1 large ripe tomato, peeled, halved, deseeded and cut into 8 wedges

2 or more red bird's eye chillies, deseeded and thinly sliced into rounds

1 tbsp fish sauce

12 fresh Thai basil leaves, freshly torn

6 fresh saw leaves, freshly torn, or 5 g/⅛ oz fresh coriander leaves

salt and pepper

Fried Garlic Oil, to garnish (see Cook's tip)

*Light fish stock*

2.8 litres/6 pints water

1.1 kg/2½ lb fish heads and bones

25 g/1 oz fresh ginger, peeled and thinly sliced

4 spring onions, trimmed and crushed

2–3 tbsp fish sauce

Sour soups are popular in South East Asia for their cooling effect. In Vietnam, this chilli-spiced fish and pineapple version has a distinct tamarind flavour. It is sipped like a beverage as a palate cleanser throughout the meal.

For the stock, put the water, fish heads and bones in a large saucepan and bring to the boil over a high heat. Reduce the heat to low–medium, then add the ginger, spring onions and fish sauce and simmer for 1½ hours, or until reduced by about half, skimming off any foam. Strain the stock, discarding the solids, and remove any fat.

Meanwhile, season the fish to taste with salt and pepper. Cover with clingfilm and refrigerate for up to 30 minutes.

Pour the stock into a medium saucepan and bring to a gentle boil over a medium heat. Reduce the heat to low–medium, then add the tamarind concentrate, pineapple, tomato, chillies and fish sauce and cook for 10 minutes. Add the fish chunks and cook for 5 minutes, or until opaque and fork-tender.

Ladle the soup into small individual bowls. Scatter over the torn basil and saw leaves and drizzle with Fried Garlic Oil to garnish. Serve immediately.

### Cook's tip

To make the Fried Garlic Oil, fry 8 finely chopped large garlic cloves in 6 tablespoons of vegetable oil in a small saucepan over medium heat for 3–5 minutes, or until golden. Store in the refrigerator for up to one week.

# Asparagus and crab soup

## *Sup cua mang tai*

Serves 6

450 g/1 lb cooked fresh crabmeat

270 g/9¹/₂ oz fresh white or green asparagus, cut into 2-cm/³/₄-inch pieces

2 large egg whites, lightly beaten

1 tbsp cornflour

2 tbsp water

salt and pepper

fresh coriander leaves, to garnish

*Chicken or crab stock*

2.8 litres/6 pints water

900 g/2 lb meaty chicken bones or crab shells

25 g/1 oz fresh ginger, peeled and thinly sliced

4 spring onions, trimmed and crushed

2–3 tbsp fish sauce

Unable to grow asparagus in Vietnam, where it is known as 'Western bamboo', the French imported brined versions, hoping to re-create *Velouté d'Asperge* or creamy asparagus soup. The resulting hybrid is this asparagus and crab combination.

For the stock, put the water and chicken bones or crab shells in a large saucepan and bring to the boil over a high heat. Reduce the heat to low–medium and add the ginger, spring onions and fish sauce, then simmer for 1¹/₂ hours, or until reduced by about half, skimming off any foam. Strain the stock, discarding the solids, and remove any fat.

Pour the stock into a medium saucepan and bring to a gentle boil over a medium heat. Reduce the heat to low–medium, then add the crabmeat and asparagus, and season to taste with salt and pepper. Cover and simmer for 5 minutes, or until the flavours have blended.

Steadily pour the egg whites into the soup, stirring a few times, and simmer for a further 1–2 minutes, or until they are fully cooked. In a ladle, stir the cornflour and water together. Lower the ladle into the soup, then stir a few times. Cook until lightly thickened.

Ladle the soup into small individual bowls and scatter over the coriander to garnish, then serve immediately.

# Beef fondue with anchovy and pineapple sauce

## *Bo nhung dam*

**Serves 6**

1 quantity Anchovy and Pineapple Sauce (see Cook's tip)

1 head tender lettuce, such as Little Gem or loose leaf, leaves separated

1 large carrot, peeled and cut into matchsticks

1 small cucumber, peeled, halved lengthways, deseeded and thinly sliced into half-rounds

12 sprigs fresh Thai basil, freshly torn

12 fresh saw leaves, freshly torn, or 12 sprigs fresh coriander, trimmed and chopped

115 g/4 oz dried rice vermicelli, soaked in water until pliable and drained

24 dried rice paper triangles

675–900 g/1 1/2–2 lb rump steak, thinly sliced

*Vinegar broth*

1 tbsp vegetable oil

1 lemon grass stalk

2 large garlic cloves, crushed

1 large shallot or 1/2 small red onion, thinly sliced

350 ml/12 fl oz rice vinegar

225 ml/8 fl oz water

50 g/1 3/4 oz palm sugar or granulated sugar

1/2 tsp toasted sesame oil

A speciality of Vietnam's cattle-raising Northern provinces, this dish is traditionally eaten on special occasions and offered at restaurants specializing in Beef Seven Ways (*Bo Bay Moon*). Beef hot pot is typically the first course.

For the vinegar broth, heat the vegetable oil in a fondue pot set in the centre of the dining table. Meanwhile, discard the bruised leaves and root end of the lemon grass stalk, then halve and crush 15–20 cm/6–8 inches of the lower stalk. Add the garlic, shallot and lemon grass to the oil and stir-fry for 5 minutes, or until fragrant and golden. Add the vinegar, water, sugar and sesame oil and boil gently.

Arrange the lettuce, carrot, cucumber, basil and saw leaves in individual piles on a large platter.

Bring a medium saucepan of water to the boil over a high heat. Put the vermicelli in a sieve. Lower the sieve into the water and cook the vermicelli for 3–5 seconds, or until al dente. Lift the sieve out and transfer the vermicelli to a serving dish.

Separate and soak 1 or 2 rice papers at a time in a large baking dish half-filled with room-temperature water for 1–2 minutes, or until pliable. Drain, then arrange overlapping next to the vegetables on the platter.

To eat, cook 2–3 slices of beef in the vinegar broth for 15–30 seconds, or until medium-rare. Take a rice paper, line it with a lettuce leaf and top with the cooked beef, followed by small amounts of the vermicelli, carrot, cucumber, basil and saw leaves. Wrap the rice paper to enclose the ingredients and dip in the sauce.

### Cook's tip

To make the Anchovy and Pineapple Sauce, put 150 g/5 oz peeled, cored, and finely chopped ripe pineapple; 6 anchovy fillets packed in oil, drained and bones removed; 1 large garlic clove, crushed and finely chopped; and 1 teaspoon granulated sugar in a mortar, then pound to a chunky paste with a pestle. Add 1 red bird's eye chilli, deseeded and finely chopped; 1 tablespoon rice vinegar; and 50 ml/2 fl oz freshly squeezed lemon juice. Pound to distribute evenly. Transfer to a serving bowl.

# Rice noodle soup with beef
## *Pho bo*

**Serves 6**

1 small–medium yellow onion, peeled, halved and thinly sliced

300 g/10½ oz beansprouts

12 sprigs fresh Thai basil, freshly torn

12 fresh saw leaves, freshly torn, or 12 sprigs fresh coriander, trimmed and chopped

4 red bird's eye chillies, deseeded and sliced into thin rounds

2 limes, each cut into 6 wedges

1 packet (450 g/1 lb) medium dried rice sticks, soaked in water until pliable and drained

450 g/1 lb rump steak, thinly sliced

Fried Shallots, to garnish (see Cook's tip)

hoisin sauce, to serve

*Beef stock*

1.8 kg/4 lb oxtail

3.8 litres/8 pints water

1 large onion, peeled

6 whole cloves

115 g/4 oz fresh root ginger, peeled, sliced and crushed

6 star anise

1 piece cassia bark or cinnamon stick, 7.5–10 cm/3–4 inches long

2 tbsp fish sauce, plus extra to taste

salt and pepper

Referred to as *Soupe Tonkinoise* by the French Colonials, *Pho* was originally considered a breakfast or snack food. Today, this sweet and savoury, fragrant soup, which 'cooks' its ingredients in the serving bowl, is also eaten for lunch or dinner.

For the stock, blanch the oxtail in a large saucepan of boiling water for 15 minutes and drain. Rinse the saucepan and return the oxtail with the measured fresh water. Bring to the boil over a high heat, then reduce the heat to low–medium. Add the whole onion studded with the cloves, and the ginger, star anise, cassia bark and fish sauce, and season to taste with salt and pepper. Simmer for 3 hours, or until reduced by about half, skimming off any foam. Strain the stock, discarding the solids, and remove any fat.

Pour the stock into a large clean saucepan and bring to a gentle boil over a medium heat. Adjust the seasoning to taste with fish sauce and add the sliced onion.

Arrange the beansprouts, basil, saw leaves, chillies and lime wedges in individual piles on a large platter.

Bring a medium saucepan of water to the boil over a high heat. Put a handful of rice sticks in a sieve. Lower the sieve into the water and cook the noodles for 5–7 seconds, or until al dente. Lift the sieve out and transfer the noodles to a large soup bowl. Repeat 5 more times for a total of 6 servings.

Top each of the 6 servings of noodles with 8 overlapping slices of the raw beef. Ladle 350 ml/12 fl oz of the stock (including some onions) over each serving.

To eat the soups, scatter over the beansprouts, basil, saw leaves, chillies and Fried Shallots, and squeeze over juice from the lime wedges to taste. Serve with hoisin sauce on the side for dipping the beef.

### Cook's tip
To make the Fried Shallots, thinly slice 8 medium–large shallots and separate the rings. Fry them in 125 ml/4 fl oz of vegetable oil in a saucepan over a medium–high heat for 3–5 minutes, until golden and crisp. Use a slotted spoon to transfer the rings to a plate lined with kitchen paper to drain.

# Rice noodle soup with prawns, squid and pork

*Hu tieu do bien*

Serves 6

1 small–medium yellow onion, peeled, halved and thinly sliced

300 g/10½ oz beansprouts

12 sprigs fresh Thai basil, freshly torn

12 fresh saw leaves, freshly torn, or 12 sprigs fresh coriander, trimmed and chopped

4 red bird's eye chillies, deseeded and sliced into thin rounds

2 limes, each cut into 6 wedges

1 packet (450 g/1 lb) medium dried rice sticks

18 small–medium raw tiger prawns, peeled and deveined

12 large scallops, halved

12 cleaned baby squid, cut into 1-cm/½-inch wide rings

Fried Garlic Oil, to taste (see page 176)

*Pork stock*

1 medium dried squid

1.3 kg/3 lb lean pork ribs, separated

1 cup pickled mooli

2 tbsp fish sauce, plus extra to taste

1 tbsp thick soy sauce (optional)

salt and pepper

This delicious soup of rice noodles with seafood and pork is a speciality of the South. The broth, made with dried squid, pork bones and pickled mooli, is sweet and savoury. Served with herbs, lime juice and sliced chillies, it offers a spicy finish.

For the pork stock, using tongs, char the dried squid over an open gas burner, turning often to avoid overburning. When cool enough to handle, peel or scrape away the charred, very thin skin.

Put the squid, pork ribs, pickled mooli, fish sauce and soy sauce, if using, in a large saucepan and bring to the boil over a high heat. Reduce the heat to low–medium and adjust the seasoning to taste with salt and pepper, then simmer for 3 hours, or until reduced by about half, skimming off any foam. Strain the stock, discarding the solids, and remove any fat.

Pour the stock into a large clean saucepan and bring to a gentle boil over a medium heat. Adjust the seasoning to taste with fish sauce and add the sliced onion.

Arrange the beansprouts, basil, saw leaves, chillies and lime wedges in individual piles on a large platter.

Bring a medium saucepan of water to the boil over a high heat. Put a handful of rice sticks in a sieve. Lower the sieve into the water and cook the noodles for 5–7 seconds, or until al dente. Lift the sieve out and transfer the noodles to a large soup bowl. Repeat 5 more times for a total of 6 servings.

In the same water, poach the prawns and scallops separately for 1 minute, or until opaque, then the squid for 30 seconds. Drain and distribute evenly between the noodle servings. Ladle about 350 ml/12 fl oz of the stock (including some onions) over each serving.

To eat the soup, scatter over the beansprouts, basil, saw leaves and chillies, then squeeze over juice from the lime wedges and drizzle with Fried Garlic Oil to taste. Adjust the seasoning with fish sauce to taste.

# Rice noodles with fried yellow fish, peanuts and herbs

## *Cha ca*

**Serves 6**

450 g/1 lb fresh bun, or ½ packet (225 g/8 oz) dried rice vermicelli, soaked in water until pliable

70 g/2½ oz rice flour or plain flour

½ tsp ground turmeric

900 g/2 lb white fish fillets, such as tilapia or flounder, cut into 2-cm/ ¾-inch cubes

vegetable oil, for deep-frying, plus 2 tbsp for stir-frying

4 spring onions, trimmed and cut into 2.5-cm/1-inch lengths

50 g/1¾ oz dry-roasted unsalted peanuts

24 fresh Thai basil leaves

24 sprigs fresh dill, trimmed

24 sprigs fresh coriander, trimmed

salt and pepper

Sweet, Sour and Spicy Fish Sauce, to serve (see page 222)

The eponymous Cha Ca Street in Hanoi's French Quarter is packed with restaurants serving this wonderful fried fish speciality. Traditionally served over fresh rice noodles called *bun*, the dish is garnished with stir-fried herbs and crushed peanuts.

If the bun has been refrigerated, reheat in boiling water for 2 seconds. Distribute the bun between 6 individual bowls. If using vermicelli, bring a medium saucepan of water to the boil over a high heat. Put a handful of vermicelli in a sieve. Lower the sieve into the water and cook the vermicelli for 3–5 seconds, or until al dente. Lift the sieve out and transfer the vermicelli to a large soup bowl. Repeat 5 more times for a total of 6 servings.

Put the flour and turmeric in a sealable plastic bag and season to taste with salt and pepper. Shake to mix well. Add the fish cubes, then seal the bag and shake to coat each fish cube evenly.

Heat enough oil for deep-frying in a wok, deep saucepan or deep-fat fryer to 180–190°C/ 350–375°F, or until a cube of bread browns in 30 seconds. Working in small batches, take a handful of fish cubes and shake off the excess flour, then lower into the hot oil. Deep-fry for 2–3 minutes, or until golden and crisp. Drain on a plate lined with kitchen paper.

Distribute the fried fish cubes evenly between each noodle serving.

Heat the remaining 2 tablespoons of oil in a pre-heated wok or frying pan over a high heat. Add the spring onions and peanuts and stir-fry for 1 minute, or until fragrant and wilted. Add the basil, dill and coriander and stir-fry for 1–2 minutes, or until just wilted. Distribute the stir-fry evenly between each serving and season to taste with Sweet, Sour and Spicy Fish Sauce.

# Spicy chicken and rice porridge with lemon grass

## Chao ga

**Serves 6**

1 lemon grass stalk

2–3 red bird's eye chillies, deseeded and sliced into thin rounds

400 g/14 oz long-grain jasmine rice

675 g/1½ lb skinless, boneless chicken, sliced

8 g/⅙ oz saw leaves, cut into thin strips, or trimmed and chopped sprigs of fresh coriander, to garnish

1 lemon or lime, sliced into 6 equal wedges, to serve

salt and pepper

### Light chicken stock

3.8 litres/8 pints water

900 g/2 lb meaty chicken bones

2 lemon grass stalks

4 spring onions, trimmed and crushed

2–3 tbsp fish sauce, plus extra to taste

Rice porridge is regarded as comfort food in Asia, where it is often recommended as a palliative when you are feeling less than fully fit. This version is uniquely Vietnamese with the use of lemon grass and hot chillies.

For the stock, put the water and bones in a large saucepan and bring to the boil over a high heat. Meanwhile, discard the bruised leaves and root ends of the lemon grass stalk, then halve and crush 15–20 cm/6–8 inches of the lower stalks. Reduce the heat to low–medium, then add the lemon grass, spring onions and fish sauce and simmer for 2½ hours, or until reduced by about half, skimming off any foam. Strain the stock, discarding the solids, and remove any fat.

Pour 2 litres/4½ pints of the stock into a medium–large saucepan and bring to the boil over a high heat. Meanwhile, discard the bruised leaves and root ends of the lemon grass stalks and finely grate 15–20 cm/6–8 inches of the lower stalks. Reduce the heat to low–medium, then add the lemon grass and chillies to the stock and simmer for 30 minutes. Season to taste with fish sauce.

Add the rice to the stock and simmer, partially covered, for 1 hour. Add the chicken, stirring to distribute evenly, and cook for a further 10 minutes. Adjust the seasoning with salt and pepper to taste.

Serve the porridge in individual bowls, garnished with the saw leaves and with juice squeezed over from the lemon wedges.

# Chicken, mint and shallot rice

## *Rau thom com ga*

In this simple, classic recipe, chicken is used to make a broth, which is then used to cook rice. The cooked chicken is then shredded and mixed back into the cooked rice with freshly chopped mint and shallots.

**Serves 6**

400 g/14 oz long-grain jasmine rice

2–3 shallots, finely chopped

15 g/¹/₂ oz fresh mint leaves, chiffonade (see Cook's tip)

Sweet, Sour and Spicy Fish Sauce, to serve (see page 222)

*Light chicken stock*

1.7 litres/3 pints water

1 chicken, weighing 900 g–1.1 kg/ 2–2¹/₂ lb

25 g/1 oz fresh ginger, peeled and thinly sliced

4 spring onions, trimmed and crushed

2–3 tbsp fish sauce

For the stock, put the water and chicken in a large saucepan and bring to the boil over a high heat. Reduce the heat to low–medium and add the ginger, spring onions and fish sauce. Simmer for 1¹/₂ hours, or until reduced by about half, skimming off any foam.

Transfer the cooked chicken to a platter and separate the meat from the bones and skin. Shred the meat and set aside. Strain the stock, discarding the solids, and remove any fat.

Put the rice in a bowl and cover with cold water. Swirl the rice to loosen any starch and drain. Repeat twice more until the water runs just clear. Transfer the rice to a large saucepan and add 700 ml/1¹/₄ pints of the stock. Cover

and bring to the boil over a high heat. Reduce the heat to medium-low and cook for 20–25 minutes, or until the stock is absorbed. Leave for 10 minutes, then fluff up the rice with a fork.

Add the shallots, mint and chicken to the rice and mix well. Serve in individual bowls, drizzled with Sweet, Sour and Spicy Fish Sauce to taste.

### Cook's tip

To chiffonade the mint, stack the mint leaves together and roll up tightly lengthways, like a cigar. Thinly slice crossways. Do this just as you are ready to add the mint to the rice, otherwise the mint may turn black.

# Crispy crêpes with beansprouts, spring onions and shiitake mushrooms

## Banh xeo cai

In this light dish, beansprouts and shiitake mushrooms are stir-fried with spring onions, then scattered across a lacy, crispy crêpe. The crêpe is then folded over the stir-fry, and eaten with lettuce leaves, carrots and cucumber.

**Makes about 18**

215 g/7½ oz plain rice flour

¼ tsp ground turmeric

125 ml/4 fl oz canned unsweetened coconut milk

vegetable oil, for frying

3 spring onions, trimmed, cut into 2.5-cm/1-inch lengths and halved lengthways

450 g/1 lb beansprouts

8–10 large fresh shiitake mushrooms, stems discarded, cut into thin strips

1 head lettuce, leaves separated

2 carrots, peeled and cut into matchsticks

1 small cucumber, peeled, halved lengthways, deseeded and thinly sliced into half-rounds

12 or more sprigs fresh mint

Sweet, Sour and Spicy Fish Sauce, to serve (see page 222)

Put the flour and turmeric in a medium bowl. Make a well in the centre and add the coconut milk. Whisk the dry and wet ingredients together until smooth. Set the batter aside.

Heat 1–2 teaspoons of oil in a preheated wok or frying pan over a high heat, then add the spring onions and stir-fry for 3 minutes, or until wilted. Transfer to a separate medium bowl. Repeat the process with the beansprouts, stir-frying for 30 seconds, or until just wilted, and then the shiitake mushrooms, stir-frying for 1–2 minutes. Toss the mushrooms with the spring onions and beansprouts in the bowl.

Heat 1 teaspoon of oil in a 20-cm/8-inch crêpe pan over a medium–high heat. Add 50 ml/ 2 fl oz of the batter while tilting and swirling the pan, working quickly to cover the surface of the pan evenly. Cook the crêpe for 3–5 minutes, or until the edge lifts and the crêpe is crisp. Spread a little of the stir-fried ingredients on one half of the crêpe but away from the edge. Fold the other half of the crêpe over the filling and transfer to a plate. Repeat with the remaining batter and stir-fried ingredients.

To eat, break off about one-quarter of the stuffed crêpe with your hand and place it in the centre of a lettuce leaf. Add a small amount each of carrots, cucumber and mint, then dip in the Sweet, Sour and Spicy Fish Sauce.

# Prawn and pork summer rolls

## Goi cuon

**Makes 12**

115 g/4 oz dried rice vermicelli, soaked in water until pliable and drained

225 g/8 oz pork fillet, in one piece

18 small–medium raw tiger prawns

1 head tender lettuce, such as Little Gem or loose leaf, leaves separated, ribs removed

1 large carrot, peeled and cut into matchsticks

1 small cucumber, peeled, halved lengthways, deseeded and thinly sliced into half-rounds

12 small, thin spring onions, trimmed, or 6 large spring onions, trimmed and halved lengthways

24 large fresh mint leaves

12 round rice papers, 20 cm/ 8 inches in diameter

Spicy Peanut Sauce, to serve (see page 224)

A restaurant favourite, these classic rolls can be made successfully at home with a little practice. They are typically dipped in Spicy Peanut Sauce to enhance the different flavours of the ingredients on the palate.

Bring a medium saucepan of water to the boil over a high heat. Put the vermicelli in a sieve. Lower the sieve into the water and cook the vermicelli for 3–5 seconds, or until al dente. Lift the sieve out and transfer the vermicelli to a large platter. Separate the noodles into 12 equal portions and cover with clingfilm until ready to use.

Using the same boiling water, cook the pork fillet for 20 minutes, or until cooked, then the prawns for 1–2 minutes, or until opaque. Drain and leave to cool. Slice the pork thinly against the grain. Peel the prawns and halve lengthways, then devein.

Arrange the lettuce leaves, carrot, cucumber, spring onions, mint leaves, vermicelli, pork slices and prawn halves in individual piles on a large platter.

Separate and soak 1 or 2 rice papers at a time in a large baking dish half-filled with room-temperature water for 1–2 minutes, or until pliable.

Set a clean tea towel on the work surface. When softened, take a rice paper and lay it flat on top of the towel. Blot the paper dry with a second clean tea towel. Working in layers and

2.5 cm/1 inch from the edge of the rice paper closest to you, overlap 3 prawn halves and top with a lettuce leaf, a portion of vermicelli, some carrot and cucumber, 2 pork slices and 2 mint leaves. Fold the bottom edge of the rice paper over the filling once tightly and fold in the sides. Add a spring onion, making sure the dark green part sticks out on one side, and roll to the end. Repeat with the remaining rice papers and filling ingredients. As you make each roll, soak another 1 or 2 rice papers.

Serve with Spicy Peanut Sauce on the side for dipping.

# Pork spring rolls

## *Cha gio*

**Makes 36**

6 fresh cloud ears, finely chopped, or dried cloud ears

55 g/2 oz dried cellophane noodles, soaked in water until pliable, drained and chopped

450 g/1 lb coarsely minced pork

1 small yellow onion, finely chopped

1 small carrot, peeled and grated

1 large egg

36 rice paper triangles, or 9 large round rice papers, 25 cm/10 inches in diameter, each quartered into triangles

vegetable oil, for deep-frying

1 head tender lettuce, such as Little Gem or loose leaf, leaves separated

1 large carrot, peeled and cut into matchsticks

1 small cucumber, peeled, halved lengthways, deseeded and thinly sliced into half-rounds

1 bunch fresh mint, leaves removed from sprigs

salt and pepper

Spicy Peanut Sauce, to serve (see page 224)

Filled with pork or a combination of pork and crab, these spring rolls are of Chinese origin. Although relatively easy to prepare, the recipe can be time-consuming, so they are generally reserved for special occasions such as Tet, the Lunar New Year.

If using dried cloud ears, soak in room-temperature water for about 30 minutes, then drain. Put the noodles, cloud ears, minced pork, onion, carrot and egg in a large bowl. Season lightly with salt and pepper and mix together thoroughly.

Separate and soak 1 or 2 rice papers at a time in a large baking dish half-filled with room-temperature water for 1–2 minutes, or until pliable.

Set a clean tea towel on the work surface. When softened, take a rice paper and lay it flat on top of the towel, with the top point closest to you. Blot the paper dry with a second clean tea towel. Put 2 tablespoons of the pork mixture 4 cm/1½ inches away from the top point, shaping the filling into a sausage. Fold the top point over the filling once tightly, fold in the sides and roll to the end. Repeat with the remaining rice papers and pork mixture. As you make each roll, soak another 1 or 2 rice papers.

Heat enough oil for deep-frying in a wok, deep saucepan or deep-fat fryer to 180–190°C/ 350–375°F, or until a cube of bread browns in 30 seconds. Deep-fry small batches of the spring rolls at a time for 3–5 minutes, or until golden and crisp, using tongs or chopsticks to turn the rolls a few times and make sure they do not stick together. Drain on a plate lined with kitchen paper.

Meanwhile, arrange the lettuce leaves, carrot, cucumber and mint in individual piles on a large platter.

To eat, put a spring roll in the centre of a lettuce leaf with some carrot and cucumber and a mint leaf. Wrap the lettuce leaf to enclose the ingredients and dip in Spicy Peanut Sauce.

# Stuffed crab shells

## *Cua farci*

**Serves 6**

8 fresh cloud ears (a Chinese fungus), finely chopped, or dried cloud ears

20 g/³/₄ oz dried cellophane noodles, soaked in water until pliable, and drained

900 g/2 lb cooked fresh crabmeat

450 g/1 lb minced pork

1 large shallot, finely chopped

1 large garlic clove, finely chopped

2 large eggs

12 Atlantic blue crab shells (about 13 cm/5 inches point to point), scrubbed clean inside and out

50 ml/2 fl oz vegetable oil

salt and pepper

**To serve**

Spring Onion Oil (see Cook's tips)

Spicy Peanut Sauce (see page 224)

Stuffed crab shells are a direct influence of the French, but with a Vietnamese twist (*farci* is French for 'stuffed'). Drizzled with Spicy Peanut Sauce, the dish is eaten with rice, and makes a great main course or starter.

If using dried cloud ears, soak in room-temperature water for about 30 minutes, then drain.

Preheat the oven to 190°C/375°F/Gas Mark 5.

Meanwhile, put the noodles, cloud ears, crabmeat, minced pork, shallot, garlic and eggs in a bowl. Season lightly with salt and pepper and mix together thoroughly.

Stuff each crab shell with the filling, making sure to distribute it equally between the shells. Brush some oil or add a sliver of butter on top of each mound of filling. Set the stuffed shells, filling-side up, on a baking sheet and bake in the preheated oven for 25–30 minutes, or until cooked through and golden.

Serve hot, drizzled with Spring Onion Oil (including spring onion pieces) and Spicy Peanut Sauce to taste.

### Cook's tips

Cellophane noodles are opaque when uncooked but transparent when cooked. They are chewy and flavourless, and are used as a filler in many Asian recipes. Rice vermicelli, often confused with cellophane noodles, can't be substituted. Do make sure to use cellophane noodles derived from Chinese mung bean starch, rather than the Japanese or Korean potato starch versions, which are much thicker.

To make the Spring Onion Oil, trim and slice a bunch of spring onions into 5 mm/¹/₄ inch thick pieces. Fry in 6 tablespoons of vegetable oil in a small saucepan over a medium heat for 2–3 minutes, or until fragrant and wilted. Store in the refrigerator for up to one week.

# Meats and Seafood

Meats and seafood are an integral part of the Vietnamese diet, and here you can sample a variety in a selection of classic dishes, from crispy fried fish fillets and quickly cooked pork fillet, to curried chicken, duck braised with orange and beef with aromatic spices.

Any of these delicious dishes can be served with rice, noodles or French baguette. For a simple lunch, select any meat, poultry or seafood recipe and combine with Pickled Vegetables or a salad such as Green Pawpaw Salad or Sweet and Sour Cabbage Salad, and serve with rice. For a more elaborate meal, choose one meat or poultry and one seafood recipe, and add stir-fried vegetables, a salad, a clear soup and plain cooked rice.

# Crispy fish with stir-fried tomatoes and herbs

## *Ca chien sot ca chua*

**Serves 6**

140 g/5 oz plain flour

6 flounder or tilapia fillets, about 175 g/6 oz each

4–6 tbsp vegetable oil

2 large garlic cloves, thinly sliced

4 ripe tomatoes, quartered

1 tbsp fish sauce

12 sprigs fresh dill, trimmed

12 sprigs fresh coriander, trimmed

12 fresh Thai basil leaves

salt and pepper

*To serve*

long-grain jasmine rice

Sweet, Sour and Spicy Fish Sauce (see page 222)

The Mekong River and its Delta are abundant with fish, and catfish is a common menu item. Fried until golden and crisp, the fish in this dish is topped with stir-fried tomatoes and garlic, and garnished with stir-fried herbs.

Put the flour and salt and pepper to taste in a sealable polythene bag. Add the fish and seal the bag, then shake to coat each fillet evenly.

Heat 2 tablespoons of oil in a frying pan over a high heat. Working in batches and replenishing the oil as necessary, fry the fillets for 5–7 minutes, or until golden and crisp on both sides. Transfer to a serving platter.

In a separate frying pan, heat 1 tablespoon of oil over a high heat, then add the garlic and stir-fry for 3–5 minutes, or until just golden. Add the tomatoes and fish sauce and stir-fry for 10 minutes, or until softened. Adjust the seasoning with salt and pepper to taste. Spoon the tomato mixture on top of the fish.

Wipe the frying pan clean and heat 1 tablespoon of oil over a high heat. Add the dill, coriander and basil and stir-fry for 1–2 minutes, or until just wilted. Scatter over the tomatoes and fish. Serve with jasmine rice and Sweet, Sour and Spicy Fish Sauce on the side.

# Prawn quenelles

## *Chao tom*

**Serves 6**

900 g/2 lb raw tiger prawns, peeled, deveined and finely chopped

70 g/2½ oz Toasted Rice Flour (see Cook's tip)

3 tbsp vegetable oil

1 tsp palm sugar or granulated sugar

1 tsp bicarbonate of soda

2 spring onions, trimmed and finely chopped

1 head tender lettuce, such as Little Gem or loose leaf, leaves separated

1 carrot, peeled and cut into matchsticks

1 small cucumber, peeled, halved lengthways, deseeded and thinly sliced into half-rounds

12 fresh mint leaves

salt and pepper

Sweet, Sour and Spicy Fish Sauce, to serve (see page 222)

Prawn quenelles are a Vietnamese classic. Fresh prawns are pounded or chopped to a fine paste consistency, and seasoned with Toasted Rice Flour and spring onions. Traditionally, the mixture is wrapped around pieces of sugar cane and grilled.

Put the prawns, 2 tablespoons of the flour, 2 tablespoons of the oil, the sugar, bicarbonate of soda and spring onions in a bowl. Season lightly with salt and pepper and mix together thoroughly.

Scatter the remaining flour on a plate. Divide the prawn mixture into 12 equal portions. Shape each into 4 cm/1½ inch long quenelle (or sausage). Roll each quenelle in the flour to coat.

Arrange the lettuce leaves, carrot, cucumber and mint leaves in individual piles on a large platter, with the Sweet, Sour and Spicy Fish Sauce in a small serving dish on the side.

Heat the remaining oil in a non-stick frying pan over a medium–high heat. Add the quenelles and fry, rolling them around, for 5 minutes, or until golden and crisp all over.

To eat, put a quenelle in the centre of a lettuce leaf with some carrot and cucumber and a mint leaf. Wrap the lettuce leaf to enclose the ingredients and dip in the Sweet, Sour and Spicy Fish Sauce.

### Cook's tip

To make the Toasted Rice Flour, toast 200 g/ 7 oz of long-grain rice in a dry frying pan over a medium heat, shaking the pan to avoid burning the grains, for 15 minutes, or until a rich golden colour. Transfer to a spice grinder and process to a fine powder. Store in a cool, dark place for up to three months.

# Pork meatballs

## *Nem nuong*

**Serves 6**

2 tsp fish sauce

1 tbsp palm sugar or granulated sugar

1 small shallot, finely chopped

1 garlic clove, finely chopped

450 g/1 lb coarsely minced pork

1 head tender lettuce, such as Little Gem or loose leaf, leaves separated

1 carrot, peeled and cut into matchsticks

1 small cucumber, peeled, halved lengthways, deseeded and thinly sliced into half-rounds

12 or more fresh mint leaves

1 tbsp vegetable oil

pepper

Spicy Peanut Sauce, to serve (see page 224)

These simple pork meatballs are seasoned with fish sauce and palm sugar, and served with Spicy Peanut Sauce, with fresh vegetables on the side. They can be served as part of a meal or as an hors d'oeuvre with cocktails.

Put the fish sauce and sugar in a bowl and whisk until the sugar is completely dissolved. Stir in the shallot and garlic, and season to taste with pepper. Add the minced pork and mix together thoroughly. Cover and chill in the refrigerator for 1 hour.

Pinch off about 1 tablespoon of the pork mixture and shape into a small meatball. Repeat with the remaining pork mixture.

Arrange the lettuce leaves, carrot, cucumber and mint leaves in individual piles on a large platter with the Spicy Peanut Sauce in a small serving dish on the side.

Heat the oil in a non-stick frying pan, then add the meatballs and cook, rolling them around, for 5 minutes, or until golden all over.

To eat, put a meatball in the centre of a lettuce leaf with some carrot and cucumber and a mint leaf. Wrap the lettuce leaf to enclose the ingredients and dip in the Spicy Peanut Sauce.

# Grilled lemon grass pork skewers

## *Suon nuong xa*

**Serves 6**

2 lemon grass stalks

50 ml/2 fl oz fish sauce

50 g/1¾ oz palm sugar or
granulated sugar

2 tbsp vegetable oil

2 large garlic cloves, finely grated

675–900 g/1½–2 lb pork fillet,
thinly sliced

### To serve

long-grain jasmine rice

Sweet, Sour and Spicy Fish Sauce
(see page 222)

The pig is prized as a productive animal in Vietnam, and is an integral part of Vietnamese cuisine. Virtually nothing is wasted: the fat is used as cooking oil, the bones are used for stock, and the meat and innards are prepared in numerous ways.

Presoak 24 or more bamboo skewers, about 20 cm/8 inches long, in water for 30 minutes.

Meanwhile, discard the bruised leaves and root ends of the lemon grass stalks, then finely grate 15–20 cm/6–8 inches of the lower stalks. Put the fish sauce and sugar in a bowl and whisk until the sugar is completely dissolved. Add the oil, lemon grass and garlic and stir well. Add the pork and mix to coat the pieces fully. Cover and leave to marinate in a cool place for 20 minutes.

Prepare an outdoor charcoal grill or preheat a grill to a medium–high heat, or preheat a non-stick griddle pan over a medium–high heat. Meanwhile, drain the skewers, then thread the marinated pork onto the skewers.

Grill the skewered pork for 1–2 minutes on each side, or until cooked and crisp. Serve with rice and Sweet, Sour and Spicy Fish Sauce.

# Braised pork shanks in caramel sauce with eggs

*Thit heo kho nuoc dua*

**Serves 6**

60 g/2¼ oz palm sugar or granulated sugar

2 tbsp water

700 ml/1¼ pints coconut water (not coconut milk) or plain water

125 ml/4 fl oz fish sauce

1.3 kg/3 lb pork shanks with rind, bone in

6 spring onions, trimmed and crushed

55 g/2 oz fresh ginger, peeled, sliced and crushed

6 large garlic cloves, crushed

4 dried red Chinese (tien sien) chillies

6 star anise

½ tsp five-spice powder

6 eggs, hard-boiled and peeled

long-grain jasmine rice, to serve

This pork dish is derived from a similar Chinese speciality. The primary differences are that the soy sauce is replaced with fish sauce, and coconut water is used instead of water. Spiced with star anise, chillies and lemon grass, this makes a hearty meal.

Cook the sugar and water in a large saucepan over a medium heat for 8 minutes, or until the sugar has melted and turned medium-brown in colour. Turn the heat off and stir in the coconut water and fish sauce.

Melt the hardened caramel over a low–medium heat. Add the pork shanks, turning to coat each piece all over with the sauce, then add the spring onions, ginger, garlic, chillies, star anise and five-spice powder. Simmer for 4 hours, or until the meat is fork-tender.

Add the eggs, turning them to coat all over with the sauce, and simmer for a further 5 minutes, or until the egg whites become a deep caramel colour. Skim the fat off the top and halve the eggs before serving on a bed of jasmine rice.

## Cook's tip

Leaner cuts of pork such as pork shoulder can be used if cut into large chunks. The gelatinous pork shank, however, is the more desirable and a classic cut for this braised dish. The eggs should be eaten in small bites with sauce to moisten their otherwise dry texture, which is the result of their having been cooked twice.

# Chicken curry

## *Cari ga*

**Serves 6**

2 lemon grass stalks

50 ml/2 fl oz vegetable oil

3 large garlic cloves, crushed

1 large shallot, thinly sliced

2 tbsp Indian curry powder

700 ml/1¼ pints canned unsweetened coconut milk

500 ml/18 fl oz coconut water (not coconut milk) or chicken stock

2 tbsp fish sauce

4 fresh red bird's eye chillies or dried red Chinese (tien sien) chillies

6 kaffir lime leaves

6 boneless chicken thighs or breasts, 175–225 g/6–8 oz each, with or without skin, cut into 5-cm/2-inch pieces

1 large white yam or sweet potato, peeled and cut into 2.5-cm/1-inch chunks

2 Asian aubergines, cut into 2.5-cm/1-inch pieces

250 g/9 oz green beans, trimmed

2 carrots, peeled and cut diagonally into 1-cm/½-inch thick pieces

long-grain jasmine rice, to serve

*To garnish*

12 fresh Thai basil leaves, lightly crushed

Fried Shallots (see page 182)

This Vietnamese curry is delicate in comparison to the more widely known Thai curries. The sweet and savoury broth is coconut milk seasoned with Indian curry powder, fish sauce and lemon grass. Fried Shallots and herbs are used as garnish.

Discard the bruised leaves and root ends of the lemon grass stalks, then slice 15–20 cm/6–8 inches of the lower stalks paper thin.

Heat the oil in a large saucepan over a high heat, then add the garlic and shallot and stir-fry for 5 minutes, or until golden. Add the lemon grass and curry powder and stir-fry for 2 minutes, or until fragrant. Add the coconut milk, coconut water, fish sauce, chillies and lime leaves and bring to the boil. Reduce the heat to low and add the chicken, yam, aubergines, green beans and carrots. Simmer, covered, for 1 hour, or until the chicken and vegetables are fork-tender and the flavours have blended.

Serve, garnished with the basil leaves and Fried Shallots, with jasmine rice on the side.

# Duck in orange sauce

*Vit nau cam*

**Serves 6**

1 tbsp vegetable oil

6 duck legs (thighs and drumsticks), 175–225 g/6–8 oz each

2 lemon grass stalks

8 large garlic cloves, crushed

55 g/2 oz fresh ginger, peeled and thinly sliced

6 spring onions, 4 trimmed and crushed, 2 trimmed and thinly sliced diagonally

1 litre/1¾ pints freshly squeezed orange juice

freshly squeezed juice of 2 limes

50 ml/2 fl oz fish sauce

1 tbsp palm sugar or granulated sugar

1 tsp five-spice powder

6 star anise

4 fresh red bird's eye chillies or dried red Chinese (tien sien) chillies

500–700 ml/18–21 fl oz water

salt and pepper

This duck dish, braised with orange juice and spices, is derived from the French classic *Canard à l'Orange*. Cooked until the meat just about falls off the bones, it is delicious served with rice and Stir-fried Leafy Greens.

Heat the oil in a large saucepan over a high heat, then add the duck legs and cook for 20 minutes, or until crisp all over, cooking the first side until crisp and coming off the base of the pan easily, then turning over and cooking the other side.

Meanwhile, discard the bruised leaves and root ends of the lemon grass stalks, then halve and crush 15–20 cm/6–8 inches of the lower stalks.

Transfer the duck legs to a plate. Drain off most of the fat from the saucepan, leaving about 1 tablespoon in the pan. Heat over a high heat, then add the garlic, ginger and crushed spring onions and stir-fry for 5 minutes, or until fragrant and golden. Add the orange juice, lime juice, fish sauce, sugar, five-spice powder, lemon grass, star anise and chillies.

Reduce the heat to low–medium and return the duck legs to the saucepan. Add enough water to cover by about 2.5 cm/1 inch. Simmer, partially covered, for 3–4 hours, or until the meat is fork-tender and falling off the bones. Adjust the seasoning with salt and pepper to taste.

Remove the fat and serve garnished with the sliced spring onions.

### Cook's tip
Beef shin is a perfect cut for braised dishes and particularly good with this spiced orange sauce. Substitute 1.3 kg/3 lb beef shin, cut into large cubes, for the duck legs. Follow the recipe, braising the meat for 4–5 hours.

# Braised beef and carrots

## *Bo kho ca rot*

**Serves 6**

100 ml/3½ fl oz fish sauce

50 g/1¾ oz palm sugar or granulated sugar

1 tsp five-spice powder

1.8 kg/4 lb beef short ribs or oxtail, or 1.3 kg/3 lb beef shin, cut into 5-cm/2-inch pieces

3 lemon grass stalks

1 tbsp vegetable oil

8 large garlic cloves, crushed

6 small–medium shallots, peeled

85 g/3 oz fresh ginger, peeled and thinly sliced

1.2 litres/2 pints coconut water (not coconut milk) or water

500–700 ml/18–21 fl oz water

6 star anise

1 piece cassia bark or cinnamon stick, about 10 cm/4 inches long

4 fresh red bird's eye chillies or dried red Chinese (tien sien) chillies

4 large carrots, peeled and cut diagonally into 1-cm/½-inch thick pieces

salt and pepper

plain boiled rice, to serve

*Boeuf aux Carrottes* was craved by the Colonial French, and their Vietnamese cooks obliged with their very own variation on the original. Seasoned with fish sauce and spiced with cassia bark, lemon grass and chillies, this dish packs a lot of heat.

Put the fish sauce and sugar in a large bowl and whisk until the sugar is completely dissolved. Add the five-spice powder and mix well. Add the meat and turn to coat evenly. Transfer the marinade and meat to a sealable polythene bag and seal the bag, then leave to marinate in the refrigerator, flipping the bag over every hour or so, for 6 hours.

Meanwhile, discard the bruised leaves and root ends of the lemon grass stalks, then halve and crush 15–20 cm/6–8 inches of the lower stalks.

Heat the oil in a large saucepan over a high heat, then add the garlic, shallots and ginger and stir-fry for 5 minutes, or until golden. Add the coconut water, water, lemon grass, star anise, cassia and chillies. Reduce the heat to low–medium and add the meat and marinade and enough water to cover by about 2.5 cm/ 1 inch. Simmer, partially covered, for 2 hours, then add the carrots. Cook for a further 2–3 hours, or until the meat is fork-tender and falls off the bones. Adjust the seasoning with salt and pepper to taste.

Remove the fat and serve on a bed of rice.

# Beef in vine leaves

## *Bo la lot*

**Makes 36**

1 lemon grass stalk

550 g/1 lb 4 oz lean beef mince

1 large shallot, finely chopped

1 large garlic clove, finely chopped

1 tbsp palm sugar or granulated sugar

1 tbsp fish sauce

36 vine leaves in brine, soaked in several changes of water and drained

2 tbsp vegetable oil, plus extra for oiling, if needed

Sweet, Sour and Spicy Fish Sauce (see page 222)

Betel leaves *(la lot)* are not widely available outside of South East Asia, but vine leaves are an acceptable substitute. Minced beef is seasoned and then wrapped in the leaves. The resulting rolls are threaded on skewers, grilled, then eaten whole.

Presoak 12 bamboo skewers, about 20 cm/8 inches long, in water for 30 minutes. (It is necessary to skewer the rolls if grilling outdoors – see Cook's tip.)

Meanwhile, discard the bruised leaves and root end of the lemon grass stalk, then finely grate 15–20 cm/6–8 inches of the lower stalk.

Put the beef mince, shallot, garlic, lemon grass, sugar and fish sauce in a bowl and mix thoroughly – it is best to mix by hand.

Lay a vine leaf flat on a clean work surface, with the pointed tip closest to you. Add about 1 tablespoon of the meat mixture 2.5 cm/1 inch from the pointed tip and shape it into a 4-cm/1½-inch long sausage. Fold the pointed tip of the leaf over the filling once, then fold in the sides and continue rolling to the end. Repeat with the remaining leaves and meat mixture.

Prepare a barbecue or preheat a grill to a medium–high heat, or brush a non-stick griddle pan and preheat over a medium–high heat. Meanwhile, drain the skewers. Holding 2 skewers parallel, thread 6 rolls onto the skewers, leaving a 3-mm/⅛-inch space in between each roll to allow the heat through when grilling. Repeat with the remaining skewers and rolls. Brush lightly with the oil.

Grill for 2 minutes each side, or until the leaves are crisp, or cook in the griddle pan (skewered or not), in batches if necessary, for 2–3 minutes each side, or until the leaves are crisp.

### Cook's tip

Flat, wide bamboo skewers are now available that will prevent the rolls from twirling around, which they sometimes do with thin, round skewers.

# Condiments and Vegetables

Condiments and vegetables form an important part of Vietnamese cuisine — a humble meal often includes rice together with pickled or stir-fried vegetables and a table sauce. Sweet, Sour and Spicy Fish Sauce (*nuoc cham*) and Spicy Peanut Sauce (*nuoc cham dau phong*) are the most popular sauces, and can be served to accompany any dish.

Vegetables are eaten fresh, but just as often pickled in rice vinegar and sugar, or freshly tossed in a sauce similar to *nuoc cham*. Unripe fruit is also enjoyed in salads, as in the refreshing Green Pawpaw Salad given here. A simple recipe for Stir-fried Leafy Greens is also included, together with Vegetable Curry and Fried Tofu with Lemon Grass.

# Sweet, sour and spicy fish sauce

## *Nuoc cham*

Makes about 500 ml/18 fl oz

175 ml/6 fl oz fish sauce

100 ml/3½ oz palm sugar or granulated sugar

175 ml/6 fl oz freshly squeezed lime or lemon juice

1 large garlic clove, crushed, sliced or finely chopped

1–2 red bird's eye chillies, deseeded and halved, or thinly sliced into rounds

The ubiquitous table condiment of Vietnam, this sauce is present at virtually every meal. It features lime juice, fish sauce and sugar, spiced with garlic and chillies. The level of spiciness depends on how these two latter ingredients are prepared.

Put the fish sauce and sugar in a non-reactive bowl and whisk until the sugar is completely dissolved in the fish sauce.

Add the lime juice, garlic and chillies. Leave to stand for 20 minutes before serving.

### Cook's tip

There are as many versions of *Nuoc Cham* as there are cooks. Some like the sauce salty, some like it sour and some like it sweet. It can also be mild or spicy. Adjust the sauce according to personal taste. Note that the more the garlic and chillies are broken down, the spicier the sauce will be; for a mild sauce, do make sure to crush, not finely chop, the garlic, and halve the chilli pod rather than slicing it into thin rounds.

# Spicy peanut sauce

## *Nuoc cham dau phong*

**Makes 350 ml/12 fl oz**

2 tbsp vegetable oil

1 large garlic clove, finely chopped

115 g/4 oz dry-roasted unsalted peanuts, ground

225 m/8 fl oz chicken stock

225 m/8 fl oz canned unsweetened coconut milk

50 ml/2 fl oz tamarind concentrate

2 tbsp fish sauce

50 ml/2 fl oz hoisin sauce

3 tbsp palm sugar or granulated sugar

2 red bird's eye chillies, deseeded and finely chopped

Peanut sauce is popular throughout South East Asia. In Vietnam, it tends to be delicate, with chicken stock and tamarind concentrate used to dilute the richness of the basic coconut milk and crushed and puréed peanuts.

Heat the oil in a small–medium saucepan over a high heat, then add the garlic and stir-fry for 3 minutes, or until golden. Add the peanuts and stir-fry for 8–10 minutes, or until slightly darker and the natural oils start to render.

Add the stock, coconut milk, tamarind concentrate, fish sauce, hoisin sauce, sugar and chillies. Bring to the boil, then reduce the heat and simmer for 30 minutes, or until reduced by about half.

### Cook's tip

For an instant Vietnamese restaurant-style peanut sauce, stir together 125 ml/4 fl oz of water, 125 ml/4 fl oz of hoisin sauce and 125 g/4 1/2 oz of pure peanut butter.

# Pickled vegetables

## *Rau cai chua*

**Serves 6**

2 large carrots, peeled and cut into matchsticks

1 small mooli (about 450 g/1 lb), peeled and thinly sliced into rounds

1 large ridged cucumber, peeled (optional), halved lengthways, deseeded and thinly sliced into half-rounds

3 tsp coarsely ground salt

225 ml/8 fl oz rice vinegar

60 g/2¼ oz palm sugar or granulated sugar

Like *Nuoc Cham*, pickled vegetables are ubiquitous in Vietnamese cuisine. A humble lunch can mean a bowl of rice topped with the popular combination of sweet-and-sour carrots, cucumber and mooli, for example.

Put the carrots, mooli and cucumber in 3 separate bowls and toss each with 1 teaspoon of the salt. Leave to stand for 1 hour, tossing occasionally, then drain.

Put the vinegar and sugar in a non-reactive bowl and whisk until the sugar is completely dissolved. Add the carrots, mooli and cucumber and toss well. Leave to stand for 1 hour, tossing occasionally, then drain before serving.

### Cook's tip

This salad is a great accompaniment to grilled meats or seafood. Store in the refrigerator for up to 2 weeks. For more elaborate, often more festive meals, pickled vegetables can be offered as delicate 'starter nibbles' to whet the appetite.

# Sweet and sour cabbage salad

*Goi cai*

Serves 6

125 ml/4 fl oz fish sauce

125 ml/4 fl oz freshly squeezed lime juice

100 g/3½ oz palm sugar or granulated sugar

2 tbsp vegetable oil

3 red bird's eye chillies, deseeded and thinly sliced into rounds

1 small green cabbage, finely shredded

2 large carrots, cut into matchsticks

1 small red onion, finely sliced

12 large fresh Thai basil leaves, freshly torn, or 8 g/⅙ oz fresh coriander leaves

In this salad, shredded cabbage and carrots are tossed in fish sauce, lime juice and sugar and spiced with chillies. It can be served on its own, or for a heartier meal, with leftover cooked and shredded chicken, poached prawns or sliced pork.

Put the fish sauce, lime juice and sugar in a non-reactive bowl and whisk until the sugar is completely dissolved. Add the oil, chillies, cabbage, carrots and onion. Toss well and leave to stand for 30 minutes to 1 hour.

Drain and serve scattered with the basil.

### Cook's tip
To liven up the dining table with vibrant colour, substitute red cabbage for the green cabbage. You can also combine half a red cabbage with half a green cabbage.

# Green pawpaw salad

## *Goi du du*

**Serves 6**

125 ml/4 fl oz freshly squeezed lime juice

100 ml/3¹/₂ fl oz fish sauce

60 g/2¹/₄ oz palm sugar or granulated sugar

1 large green pawpaw, peeled, deseeded and cut into very thin matchsticks

2 small carrots, peeled and cut into matchsticks

3 red bird's eye chillies, deseeded and thinly sliced into rounds

75 g/2³/₄ oz dry-roasted, unsalted peanuts, chopped

8 g/¹/₆ oz fresh coriander leaves, or 12 fresh Thai basil leaves, freshly torn

Green pawpaw salad is served throughout Vietnam. Tossed with a sweet-and-sour fish-sauce-based dressing, it is wonderfully refreshing. The basic salad is finished with crushed peanuts and Thai basil (or coriander), and offers spicy flavour notes.

Put the lime juice, fish sauce and sugar in a non-reactive bowl and whisk until the sugar is completely dissolved. Add the pawpaw, carrots and chillies. Toss well and leave to stand for 30 minutes.

Drain and serve scattered with the peanuts and coriander.

### Variation
Green mango is a popular substitute for the pawpaw and is equally delicious when prepared in the same style.

# Stir-fried leafy greens

## Cai xao

**Serves 6**

2 tbsp vegetable oil

2 large garlic cloves, thinly sliced

675–900 g/1¹/₂–2 lb leafy green vegetables, such as spinach or baby pak choi, leaves separated

fish sauce, to taste

pepper

Spinach, pak choi or Chinese broccoli is stir-fried with oil and flavoured with garlic and fish sauce in this simple vegetable dish. However, water spinach is the most typical Vietnamese leafy green vegetable.

Heat the oil in a wok or large frying pan over a high heat, then add the garlic and stir-fry for 3 minutes, or until golden.

Add the leafy green vegetables and stir-fry for 2–4 minutes, or until wilted (spinach) and tender (pak choi). Season to taste with fish sauce and pepper.

### Cook's tip

Try the recipe with Asian leafy greens, such as water spinach, which has long, narrow, pointed leaves and hollow stems, or chrysanthemum leaves, which are long and narrow-lobed. Sliced Chinese broccoli can also be stir-fried in the same fashion. If you like a crunchy texture, try sugar snap peas or runner beans. If you feel inspired, add 85 g/3 oz shiitake mushroom caps cut into thin strips to the mix.

# Vegetable curry

## *Cari cai*

**Serves 6**

2 lemon grass stalks

50 ml/2 fl oz vegetable oil

3 large garlic cloves, crushed

1 large shallot, thinly sliced

2 tbsp Indian curry powder

700 ml/1¼ pints canned unsweetened coconut milk

500 ml/18 fl oz coconut water (not coconut milk) or vegetable stock

2 tbsp fish sauce

4 fresh red bird's eye chillies or dried red Chinese (tien sien) chillies

6 kaffir lime leaves

1 carrot, peeled and cut diagonally into 1-cm/½-inch thick pieces

1 small–medium Asian aubergine, cut into 2.5-cm/1-inch pieces

1 small–medium bamboo shoot, cut into thin wedges

115 g/4 oz sugar snap peas, trimmed

12 large shiitake mushrooms, stems discarded, caps halved

450 g/1 lb firm or extra-firm tofu, drained and cut into 2.5-cm/1-inch cubes

### To garnish

12 fresh Thai basil leaves, lightly crushed, or 8 g/⅙ oz fresh coriander leaves

Fried Shallots (see page 182)

Curries are popular in South Vietnam, where Indian-influenced spicy foods are enjoyed. This vegetable and tofu curry can be served with French baguette (the classic way), rice or noodles.

Discard the bruised leaves and root ends of the lemon grass stalks, then slice 15–20 cm/6–8 inches of the lower stalks paper thin.

Heat the oil in a large saucepan over a high heat, add the garlic and shallot and stir-fry for 5 minutes, or until golden. Add the lemon grass and curry powder and stir-fry for 2 minutes, or until fragrant. Add the coconut milk, coconut water, fish sauce, chillies and lime leaves and bring to the boil. Reduce the heat to low, then add the carrot and aubergine, cover and cook for 10 minutes.

Add the bamboo shoot, sugar snap peas, mushrooms and tofu and cook for a further 5 minutes.

Serve, garnished with the basil leaves and Fried Shallots.

### Cook's tip
Boiled and vacuum-packed whole bamboo shoots from Japan are the best. These can be sliced and used without any further preparation. If using fresh bamboo, be sure to peel and boil the shoot for 10 minutes in water before using in the recipe. If using frozen raw bamboo, do the same. If using canned bamboo, make sure to use a whole shoot instead of precut shoots. Bamboo shoots have the ability to absorb flavour. For this reason, canned bamboo must be boiled for 2 minutes to eliminate any flavour from the can.

# Fried tofu with lemon grass

## Dau hu xao xa

**Serves 6**

3 tbsp fish sauce

3 tbsp freshly squeezed lime or lemon juice

3 tbsp palm sugar or granulated sugar

1 lemon grass stalk

vegetable oil, for frying

1 large shallot, finely chopped

1 large garlic clove, finely chopped

1 red bird's eye chilli, deseeded and finely chopped

900 g/2 lb firm or extra-firm tofu, drained and cut crossways into 1-cm/½-inch thick rectangular slices

6 sprigs fresh coriander, trimmed, to garnish

Tofu was brought to Vietnam from China. It is eaten in soups, braised or fried, such as in this delicious version topped with a stir-fry of lemon grass, shallots, garlic and chilli.

Put the fish sauce, lime juice and sugar in a non-reactive bowl and whisk until the sugar is completely dissolved. Reserve.

Discard the bruised leaves and root end of the lemon grass stalk, then finely grate 15–20 cm/6–8 inches of the lower stalk.

Heat 2 tablespoons of oil in a small saucepan over a high heat, then add the lemon grass, shallot, garlic and chilli and stir-fry for 5 minutes, or until fragrant and golden. Transfer to the fish sauce mixture and stir well. Reserve.

Working in batches if necessary, heat 2 tablespoons of oil in a non-stick frying pan, then add the tofu slices and fry over a high heat, turning often, for 6 minutes, or until golden and crisp on both sides. Drain on a plate lined with kitchen paper. If cooking in batches, add extra oil to the frying pan as needed.

Transfer the fried tofu to a serving platter and spoon the herb sauce over each slice, then garnish with the coriander sprigs.

# Sweets and Drinks

Sweet or dessert items are not traditionally served at the end of a meal in Vietnam. Asian cuisines are characterized by a five-flavour system of sour, sweet, salty, spicy and bitter notes, and in Vietnamese cooking, sugar is present throughout most meals, so serving a cake as a finale is considered unnecessary. Instead, fresh fruit is eaten to aid digestion.

The dishes in this chapter are served as snacks, often in the afternoon with tea or coffee. Banana is a favoured ingredient, paired here with coconut in a sweet tapioca soup, as well as coated whole with batter, deep-fried and then flambéed. Coconut features again in a colourful drink and is combined with shredded cassava root for a sticky cake.

# Banana and coconut tapioca

## *Che chuoi*

**Serves 6**

700 ml/1¼ pints canned unsweetened coconut milk

700 ml/1¼ pints water

60 g/2¼ oz palm sugar or granulated sugar

½ tsp salt

½ cup small tapioca pearls

2 ripe bananas, peeled, quartered lengthways and cut into 1-cm/ ½-inch dice

toasted sesame seeds, to decorate

A popular dessert throughout South East Asia, this banana and coconut tapioca soup is simple to make. The soup may be thick or thin, depending on the amount of tapioca used. It can also be served hot, at room temperature, or lightly chilled.

Pour the coconut milk and water into a medium–large saucepan and bring to the boil over a high heat. Reduce the heat to low and add the sugar and salt. While stirring, sprinkle the tapioca pearls into the saucepan in a steady stream. Cook, stirring to keep the pearls from clumping together, for 30 minutes, or until cooked through and fully transparent.

Turn off the heat and add the bananas, then cover. Leave the bananas to steam for about 10 minutes.

Serve hot, at room temperature, or lightly chilled in individual bowls, lightly decorated with toasted sesame seeds.

# Mung bean soup

## *Che dau xanh*

**Serves 6**

225 g/8 oz peeled dried yellow split mung beans, soaked in water for 3 hours, then drained

1 litre/1³/4 cups canned unsweetened coconut milk

60 g/2¹/4 oz palm sugar or granulated sugar

¹/2 tsp salt

toasted sesame seeds, to decorate

Here, dried yellow split mung beans are cooked and puréed, then whisked into palm sugar-sweetened coconut milk. The resulting delicate yellow soup is generally served hot, and is usually enjoyed as breakfast or as an afternoon snack.

Put the mung beans in a medium saucepan with enough water to cover by 1 cm/¹/2 inch and bring to the boil over a high heat. Reduce the heat to medium and cook, stirring occasionally, for 20–25 minutes, or until the water is completely absorbed by the beans.

Transfer the beans to a fine mesh sieve set over a bowl. With the back of a spoon, press the beans through the sieve. The result should be a very smooth paste.

Pour the coconut milk into a medium saucepan and bring to a gentle boil over a medium heat. Add the mung bean paste, palm sugar and salt, and whisk to a smooth consistency. Cook for 5 minutes, or until heated through.

Serve in individual bowls, lightly decorated with toasted sesame seeds.

# Fried banana dumplings

## *Chuoi chien*

**Serves 6**

vegetable oil, for deep-frying

140 g/5 oz plain flour

2 tbsp palm sugar or granulated sugar

1/2 tsp salt

2 tsp baking powder

2 large eggs

350 ml/12 fl oz canned unsweetened coconut milk

12 small, ripe Asian bananas, peeled

6 tbsp 100%-proof rice alcohol or rum (optional)

### To decorate

icing sugar

toasted sesame seeds

A direct take on the French *Bananes Flambées*, fried bananas can be served hot out of the frying oil and drained, or flambéed with rice alcohol or rum. Icing sugar and toasted sesame seeds complete the dish.

Heat enough oil for deep-frying in a wok, deep saucepan or deep-fat fryer to 180–190°C/ 350–375°F, or until a cube of bread browns in 30 seconds.

Meanwhile, put the flour, sugar, salt and baking powder in a medium–large bowl. Whisk to combine the ingredients. Make a well in the centre and add the eggs and coconut milk. Whisk, gradually incorporating the dry ingredients into the wet ingredients, until the batter is smooth. Add the bananas to the batter, making sure they are coated evenly all over.

Working in batches if necessary, lower the bananas into the hot oil and deep-fry for 5–7 minutes, or until golden and crisp all over. Drain on a plate lined with kitchen paper. Arrange 2 bananas on each individual dessert plate.

To flambé, fill a tablespoon with rice alcohol and set aflame with a match. Scatter the burning alcohol across a serving of bananas. Repeat for each serving, letting the alcohol burn off while the flames dissipate. Decorate with a light sprinkling of icing sugar and toasted sesame seeds before serving.

# Coconut yucca cake

## *Banh khoai mi*

Makes one 30 x 23-cm/
12 x 9-inch cake

butter, for greasing
500 ml/18 fl oz canned
unsweetened coconut milk
250 g/9 oz palm sugar or
granulated sugar
1/2 tsp salt
900 g/2 lb cassava root, bark
removed, shredded

South East Asian desserts often contain coconut palm sugar and coconut milk because coconut palm is abundant throughout the region. Here, coconut milk, palm sugar and shredded cassava are combined and baked into a rich, sticky cake.

Preheat the oven to 190°C/375°F/Gas Mark 5. Generously grease a 30 x 23-cm/12 x 9-inch square baking dish with butter.

Put the coconut milk, sugar and salt in a bowl and whisk until the sugar is completely dissolved. Add the cassava and stir to mix thoroughly.

Pour the cake mixture into the prepared dish, spreading it equally throughout. Bake in the preheated oven for 1¼ hours, or until golden brown. Leave to cool before slicing into approximately 5-cm/2-inch squares.

### Cook's tip
Use a glass baking dish to make sure the cake is browned all round.

# Rainbow coconut drink with mango

## Che ba mau

### Serves 6

175 g/6 oz dried adzuki beans, soaked in water for 4 hours and drained

175 g/6 oz peeled dried yellow split mung beans, soaked in water for 3 hours and drained

700 ml/1¼ pints canned unsweetened coconut milk

100–125 g/3½–4 oz palm sugar or granulated sugar

1 tsp salt

1 large ripe mango, peeled, stoned and diced

toasted sesame seeds, to decorate

crushed ice, to serve

This filling, colourful drink is made with layers of white coconut milk, red adzuki beans, yellow mung beans and ripe, diced orange mango. It makes for a great afternoon snack and is generally served with crushed or shaved ice.

Put the adzuki beans with water to cover by 5 cm/2 inches in a medium saucepan and bring to the boil over a high heat. Reduce the heat to medium and cook, stirring occasionally, for 2 hours, or until the water is completely absorbed by the beans and the beans are cooked through and tender.

Meanwhile, put the mung beans with water to cover by 1 cm/½ inch in a separate medium saucepan and bring to the boil over a high heat. Reduce the heat to medium and cook, stirring occasionally, for 20–25 minutes, or until the water is completely absorbed by the beans.

Put the coconut milk in a small saucepan and bring to the boil over a high heat. Reduce the heat to low–medium and stir in the sugar and salt.

To assemble the drink, in individual parfait glasses, and in this order, layer 2–3 tablespoons each of coconut milk, adzuki beans, crushed ice, coconut milk, mung beans, crushed ice, coconut milk and mango. Decorate with a light sprinkling of toasted sesame seeds. Serve with a long-stem spoon.

# Sweet milk coffee

## *Ca phe*

**Serves 6**

6 tbsp canned sweetened condensed milk, or to taste

6 hot double espressos or strong-brewed Thai coffees

ice cubes, to serve (optional)

Condensed milk and strong, dark-roast, espresso-like coffee are stirred together and served hot or iced. Popular throughout South East Asia, each cup is made using a single serving, slow-drip French coffee press placed over a coffee cup.

Put a heaped tablespoon of condensed milk (or more to taste) in each of 6 cups. Pour a hot double shot of espresso into each cup and stir.

For iced coffee, half-fill 6 tall glasses with ice cubes. Pour one cup of stirred espresso and condensed milk over the ice in each glass.

### Variation
Substitute strong-brewed black tea (such as gunpowder tea) for the coffee and follow the recipe to make condensed milk-sweetened tea.

# Latin

The continent of South America is vast and the lands of the Latins –
the regions colonized by Spain and Portugal – stretch from the steamy
tropics to the polar ice cap.

Latin American cuisine offers an enticing combination of native culinary
traditions and Spanish and Portuguese influences. With a wide range
of ingredients available in a region that varies from sea to mountains
and from rainforests to deserts, the result is a cuisine that is fresh
and delicious.

# Appetizers and Snacks

Throughout the region, the menu of the day is not so much a series of
main events as several moments that bridge the gap between the dawn
to midday period, when heavy bean and grain dishes are traditionally
served, and dusk, when something light is eaten.

Among those dishes that are regarded as snacks to be eaten during the
day as well as being suitable to serve as starters are the classic *seviche*,
marinated raw fish, and *escabeche*, fried fish pickled in a spiced vinegar.
Then there are foods that can be held in the hand, such as the ever-
popular *quesadillas* and *empanadas*, offering delicious fillings encased
in crisp pastry parcels. Also included are simple stock-based soups.

# Lime-marinated swordfish with prawns

## *Seviche de pez-espada con camarones*

The fish and shellfish effectively 'cook' in the citrus juice in which they are marinated, without the application of heat – a method also used by the fishermen of the South Seas, early colonizers of America's Pacific coastline.

**Serves 4–6**

350 g/12 oz swordfish steaks

250 g/9 oz raw prawns

juice of 3 limes

1 tsp sea salt

2 tbsp roughly chopped fresh coriander leaves

1 green or red chilli, deseeded and finely chopped

2 tbsp diced pawpaw or avocado (optional)

### *To serve*

lime quarters

unsalted tortilla chips or soft cornmeal tortillas

Remove the skin and bones from the fish steaks. Cut the fish into neat, bite-sized pieces, removing any stray bones, and transfer to a non-reactive bowl.

Remove the heads and tails of the prawns, then peel. If large, remove the black intestinal vein that runs down the back by pulling on the centre of the tail fin. Save the shells for making a stock.

Add the prawns to the fish with two-thirds of the lime juice and the salt and gently combine. Cover the bowl with clingfilm and leave to marinate in the salad compartment of the refrigerator for 2–3 hours, or until the fish and shellfish are opaque.

Drain, discarding the juices, and dress with the remaining lime juice, coriander and chilli. Fold in the pawpaw, if using.

Serve at room temperature with lime quarters and unsalted tortilla chips, or soft tortillas cut into bite-sized triangles or squares and fried in a little vegetable oil until crisp.

# Spice-pickled bonito or tuna

*Escabeche de bonito o atún*

A herby pickling vinegar adds flavour and a little shelf life to the fisherman's catch. The technique was developed in the days when refrigeration wasn't an option, but the result tasted so good that the recipe has stayed on the menu.

**Serves 4–6**

500 g/1 lb 2 oz bonito or tuna steaks (or any firm-fleshed fish)

2 tbsp plain flour

2–3 tbsp olive oil

salt and pepper

## Marinade

1 onion, finely sliced

1 garlic clove, crushed

1 small carrot, scraped and diced

1 tbsp dried oregano, crumbled

1 tsp coriander seeds, roughly crushed

1 fresh or dried red chilli, deseeded and chopped

4 tbsp wine vinegar or lemon juice

## To serve

500 g/1 lb 2 oz fresh or canned red peppers

1–2 tbsp olive oil

crisp lettuce leaves

soft cornmeal tortillas or arepas (Chilean tortillas)

Remove the skin and bones from the fish steaks. Cut the fish into neat strips, removing any stray bones, and transfer to a non-reactive bowl. Sprinkle lightly with salt, cover and leave to stand at room temperature for 10 minutes to firm up. Drain off any liquid.

Spread the flour on a plate and season to taste with salt and pepper. Flip the fish strips through the seasoned flour.

Heat the oil in a large frying pan until hot, add a few strips of the fish and cook over a medium–high heat, turning once, for 1–2 minutes – just long enough to brown the coating and firm the flesh. Carefully transfer the strips to a shallow dish, arranging them in a single layer. Repeat until all the fish strips are cooked.

Reheat the pan with its oily juices, add the onion, garlic and carrot and cook over a medium heat, stirring, for a few moments to blend the flavours. Add the oregano, coriander, chilli, vinegar and a splash of water.

Bubble fiercely for a few minutes to soften the vegetables, then pour the contents of the frying pan over the fish and turn gently in the vinegar mixture. Cover the dish with clingfilm and leave to marinate in a cool place for at least 4 hours, or preferably overnight.

Meanwhile, prepare the red peppers. If fresh, preheat the oven to 230°C/450°F/Gas Mark 8, put on a baking tray and roast for 10–15 minutes, or until the flesh is tender and the skins are black and blistered in places. Transfer to a polythene bag and leave to stand for 10 minutes to loosen the skins. Remove the skins and seeds. Cut the flesh into strips and dress with the oil. If canned, drain, cut into strips and dress with the oil.

Scatter the red pepper strips over the fish and serve with cos lettuce leaves and soft tortillas or arepas for scooping.

# Cheese turnovers with chilli sauce

## *Quesadillas*

Serves 4–6

vegetable oil, for frying or oiling
milk, for brushing (optional)

### Pastry

350 g/12 oz strong white flour,
plus extra for dusting

1/2 tsp salt

4 tbsp olive oil

about 150 ml/5 fl oz hot water

### Filling

4 tbsp grated queso Oaxaca or
Gruyère cheese

150 g/5 1/2 oz requesón or ricotta
cheese

1 tsp finely chopped green chilli

1 tbsp chopped fresh coriander

### Chilli sauce

500 g/1 lb 2 oz fresh ripe tomatoes,
peeled and diced, or canned
chopped tomatoes

1 fresh or dried red chilli, deseeded
and chopped

1 garlic clove, chopped

1 tbsp olive oil

Here, creamy little mouthfuls of cheese are enclosed in a crisp pastry coating.
The pastry, made with hot water and olive oil, is robust enough to withstand frying,
but it can be baked instead.

First make the pastry. Sift the flour and salt into a bowl. Using your hand, work in the oil and enough hot water to make a fairly soft, smooth dough that comes away from the side of the bowl. Alternatively, use a food processor to make the dough. Form the dough into a ball, wrap in clingfilm and leave to rest in a cool place for 30 minutes.

Meanwhile, make the filling and prepare the sauce. Mash the cheeses together with the chilli and coriander in a separate bowl and set aside. Put all the sauce ingredients in a blender or food processor and blend to a purée. Transfer to a small saucepan and leave to bubble for 10 minutes, or until you have a thick dipping sauce. Set aside to cool.

Turn the pastry out onto a floured board, roll it into a sausage shape and cut into 12 equal-sized pieces. With the tips of your fingers, knead each piece into a small ball. Roll or pat each ball into a thin round the size of a large saucer – you will find the pastry easier to roll if you sandwich it between 2 sheets of clingfilm.

Drop a teaspoon of the filling off-centre onto each round, leaving a wide margin all round. Make a dip in the centre of the filling and add a dab of the sauce. Dampen the edge of each round, fold in half to enclose the filling and press the edges together to seal.

When all the quesadillas are prepared, heat a finger's depth of oil in a large frying pan over a medium–high heat. When hot, add the quesadillas, in small batches, to the oil and cook for 2 minutes on each side, or until crisp and brown. Remove and drain on kitchen paper.

Alternatively, to bake the quesadillas, preheat the oven to 190°C/375°F/Gas Mark 5. Arrange in neat lines on an oiled baking tray, brush the tops with a little milk and prick with a fork. Bake in the preheated oven for 15–20 minutes, or until well puffed and golden.

Serve the quesadillas hot, while the filling is still creamy and runny, with the extra sauce as a dip.

# Crab and chilli pasties

## *Empanadas de cangrejo*

**Serves 4–6**

vegetable oil, for oiling
milk, for brushing

### Filling

250 g/9 oz prepared fresh crabmeat
2 tbsp olive oil
2 garlic cloves, chopped
2 green chillies, deseeded
and chopped
1 green pepper, deseeded
and diced
2 tbsp diced tomato or
1 tbsp tomato purée
1 tbsp stoned olives, chopped

### Pastry

275 g/9¾ oz strong white flour,
plus extra for dusting
1 tsp baking powder
½ tsp salt
100 g/3½ oz lard, chilled and diced
1 large egg
1 egg yolk

### To serve (optional)

1 ripe avocado, stoned, peeled
and mashed
juice of 1 lime
1 tbsp chopped fresh coriander

These crisp, lard-shortened pastry parcels contain fresh-picked crabmeat – spider crabs are perfect – flavoured with garlic, chilli and olives. You can use ready-made pastry if you prefer.

First make the filling. Pick over the crabmeat and remove any stray pieces of shell. Heat the oil in a frying pan, add the garlic, chillies and green pepper and cook over a medium heat, stirring frequently, for 4–5 minutes, or until the vegetables are softened. Add the tomato and heat until bubbling, mashing to blend. Stir in the crabmeat and olives and bubble up again. Set aside to cool while you make the pastry.

Sift the flour, baking powder and salt into a large bowl. With a sharp knife, chop the lard into the flour until it resembles rough oatmeal. Beat the egg and egg yolk together with a fork, then work lightly into the flour mixture with the knife or your fingertips, adding enough cold water to make a fairly soft, smooth dough. Alternatively, use a food processor to make the dough. Form the dough into a ball and brush the outside with oil or wrap in clingfilm. Leave to rest in a cool place for 30 minutes.

Preheat the oven to 190°C/375°F/Gas Mark 5. Roll the dough out on a floured board to a thickness of about 5mm/¼ inch. Use a wine glass to cut out small rounds – choose the size you want. Put a dab of the crab mixture on each round. Dampen the edge of each round, fold in half to enclose the filling and press the edges together to seal. Arrange in neat lines on an oiled baking tray, brush the tops with milk and prick with a fork.

Bake in the preheated oven for 15–20 minutes, or until crisp and golden. If you like, serve with a dipping salsa of the avocado mixed with the lime juice and coriander.

# Potato cakes with peanut salsa

## Llapingachos con ají de maní

**Serves 4–6**

4 large floury potatoes, scrubbed and quartered

2 tbsp grated Cheddar-type cheese

2 tbsp finely chopped fresh coriander

1 red or green chilli, deseeded and finely chopped

1 large egg, beaten

vegetable oil, for frying

salt

**Peanut salsa**

250 g/9 oz roasted peanuts or coarse peanut butter

2 tbsp lemon juice

1 tsp unrefined cane sugar

4 yellow or red chillies, deseeded

1 red pepper, deseeded and chopped

2 tbsp ricotta cheese

1/2 tsp salt

Ecuadorian fast food, these little potato cakes have a satisfyingly rough texture that works perfectly with the grainy, nut-thickened dipping sauce called *ají de maní*.

Cook the potatoes in their skins in a large saucepan of salted boiling water for 20 minutes, or until tender. Drain, reserving about 150 ml/ 5 fl oz of the cooking water. As soon as the potatoes are cool enough to handle, remove the skins. Reserve two of the potato quarters, then mash the remainder roughly with a fork in a bowl. Using your hands but without crushing out all the lumps, work in the cheese, coriander, chilli, egg and a little salt.

Put all the salsa ingredients in a blender or food processor with the reserved potato and cooking water and blend to a purée. Transfer to a saucepan and heat gently until bubbling.

When ready to cook, heat a finger's depth of oil in a large frying pan over a medium–high heat. When hot, gently drop tablespoonfuls of the potato cake mixture, in small batches, into the oil, flatten with the back of the spoon and cook until the undersides are golden and crisp. Turn carefully and cook on the other side. Remove and drain on kitchen paper.

Serve the potato cakes hot, with the salsa separately for dipping, or drop a teaspoon of the sauce on top of each potato cake.

# Potato polenta bread with pine kernels

## *Chapale chileno*

This Chilean spoon bread, thickened with potato and enriched with cheese and pine kernels, is baked in a roasting tin and eaten with a shake of chilli sauce.

**Serves 4–6**

butter or lard, for greasing

1 kg/2 lb 4 oz floury potatoes, scrubbed

100 g/3¹/₂ oz ground polenta (cornmeal)

4 tbsp grated Cheddar-type cheese

2 tbsp toasted pine kernels

1 tsp dried chilli flakes

1 large egg, beaten

salt

chilli sauce, to serve

Preheat the oven to 180°C/350°F/Gas Mark 4. Grease a rectangular roasting tin with butter or lard.

Cook the potatoes in their skins in a large saucepan of salted boiling water for 20 minutes, or until tender. Drain, reserving the cooking water. As soon as the potatoes are cool enough to handle, remove the skins. Mash the potatoes roughly with a fork in a bowl. Using your hands but without crushing out all the lumps, work in the polenta, cheese, most of the pine kernels, chilli flakes, egg, a little salt and enough of the reserved cooking water to make a fairly soft dough.

Spread the dough out in the prepared tin and level off the top. Sprinkle with the remaining pine kernels, pressing them lightly into the surface. Bake in the preheated oven for 45–50 minutes, or until the top is brown and crisp and the dough is firm. Cut into squares and eat with a shake of chilli sauce.

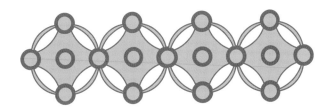

# Peanut soup

## *Chupe de maní*

**Serves 4–6**

2 tbsp groundnut oil

1 onion, finely chopped

1 floury potato, peeled and diced

1 red pepper, deseeded and
finely chopped

2 dried red chillies, deseeded
and crumbled

1 litre/1³/4 pints concentrated
chicken or beef stock

4 tbsp finely ground toasted
peanuts, plus extra peanuts to serve

salt and pepper

*To serve*

2 tbsp chopped fresh coriander

diced tomato

This is a simple, quickly prepared soup popular in Ecuador and Bolivia, where the peanut, a food crop cultivated by the Incas, remains a major source of protein.

Heat the oil in a heavy-based saucepan over a medium heat, add the onion, potato and red pepper and cook, stirring frequently, for 5 minutes, or until softened but not browned.

Stir in the chillies, add the stock and bring to the boil. Reduce the heat and simmer gently for 15 minutes, or until well blended. Transfer half the soup to a blender or food processor, add the ground toasted peanuts and blend to a purée. Stir back into the saucepan.

Taste and adjust the seasoning, then reheat gently. Ladle into bowls, top with a sprinkling of chopped coriander, diced tomato and extra peanuts and serve.

# Jerusalem artichoke soup with sweetcorn

## *Chupe de topinambures con elote*

In this elegant soup, tender sweetcorn kernels underline the sweet earthiness of the knobbly Jerusalem artichoke tubers. The Jerusalem or root artichoke is a member of the sunflower family and native to the Americas; it is no relation of the leaf artichoke.

**Serves 4–6**

500 g/1 lb 2 oz young Jerusalem artichokes

150 g/5½ oz fresh sweetcorn kernels

1 litre/1¾ pints chicken or vegetable stock

salt

*To serve*

2 tbsp crumbled feta-type crumbly salty white cheese, for sprinkling

2–3 fresh basil sprigs, leaves stripped from the stalks and torn

1 green chilli, deseeded and finely chopped

fresh bread

Scrub the artichokes – there is no need to peel them – and put in a large saucepan with enough water to cover. Add salt to taste. Bring to the boil, then reduce the heat and cook until tender – test with a fork after 20 minutes. Drain, and leave to cool. When cool enough to handle, rub off the skins, or leave with the skins on, as you prefer.

Put the sweetcorn kernels in a saucepan with enough unsalted water to cover. Bring to the boil, then reduce the heat and cook for 2–3 minutes to soften the skins. Drain, reserving the cooking water.

Put the artichokes in a blender or food processor with half the sweetcorn kernels and their cooking water and add the stock, then blend to a purée. Taste and add more salt if needed, then reheat gently in a saucepan.

Ladle into bowls and top with a sprinkling of the feta-type cheese, torn basil leaves, finely chopped chilli and the remaining sweetcorn kernels. Serve with fresh bread.

# Pinto bean soup with squid

## Sopa seca de frijoles con calamares

*Sopa seca*, or 'dry soup', is a broth-based dish that is drier than a soup but wetter than a stew. In this Mexican recipe, the broth is the cooking liquid from the squid. Seafood and beans is a popular combination throughout the whole region.

**Serves 4–6**

250 g/9 oz small squid, cleaned

2–3 tbsp olive oil

1 small onion, roughly chopped

4–5 garlic cloves, chopped

1 green chilli, deseeded and diced

2 tbsp chopped fresh epazote, or 2 tbsp chopped fresh dill and 1 tsp fennel seeds

100 ml/3½ fl oz dry sherry or white wine

500 g/1 lb 2 oz cooked drained pinto or borlotti beans

**To serve (optional)**

soft cornmeal tortillas

Rinse the squid and neatly slice if large (include the tentacles, running your fingers down the inner surface of each one to remove the little round 'toenails').

Heat the oil in a saucepan, add the onion, garlic, chilli and epazote and cook over a medium heat, stirring, for 1–2 minutes. Add the sherry and leave to bubble for 2–3 minutes, or until the alcohol evaporates. Add the squid and cook, stirring, for 2–3 minutes, or until it turns opaque – don't overcook, or it will become rubbery. Remove the squid with a slotted spoon and set aside.

Add the beans to the juices in the saucepan and simmer for 5 minutes to marry the flavours. Return the squid to the saucepan and remove from the heat. Taste and add salt (no pepper is needed, as the chilli is quite fiery enough).

Ladle into bowls and serve. If you like, serve with soft tortillas, cut into bite-sized triangles or squares and fried in a little vegetable oil until crisp, or wrapped in foil and warmed in a low oven.

# Main Courses

The main meal is taken after the end of the working day in the early afternoon, allowing time to digest substantial dishes based on pulses and grains, the subsistence foods of the region. In the city as well as rural areas, work begins soon after dawn and continues until it is time to return home for *merienda* at around one or two o'clock.

The rest of the day is a time for rest and enjoyment, with a light evening meal taken late. Robust bean dishes or a heavy roasts are only served for lunch, while dishes that fall in between may be served both in the evening and also for lunch. Fish and vegetable dishes make an appearance as a main course in the evening or a first course for lunch.

# Chicken with almonds

## *Pollo en pepián*

**Serves 4–6**

1 chicken, weighing 2 kg/4 lb 8 oz, cut into 12 neat pieces

lard, for frying

1 thick slice day-old bread, cut into cubes

2 garlic cloves, chopped

2 tbsp chopped fresh coriander

2 tbsp toasted blanched almonds

1 tsp freshly crushed allspice berries

1 tsp ground cinnamon

6 saffron strands, soaked in 1 tbsp boiling water, or 1 tsp ground turmeric

finely grated rind and juice of 1 lemon

150 ml/5 fl oz dry white wine

1 onion, finely chopped

In this fragrant dish, chicken pieces are cooked in a sauce thickened with ground almonds and flavoured with allspice and saffron.

Wipe the chicken pieces and trim off any flaps of skin.

Heat the lard in a frying pan, add the bread and the garlic and cook over a medium heat, turning once, for 4–5 minutes, or until both are golden.

Toss in the coriander and cook, stirring, for a few seconds. Remove with a slotted spoon and transfer to a blender or food processor, or a mortar, with the almonds, allspice, cinnamon, saffron and its soaking water, lemon rind and juice and wine. Blend or pound with a pestle to a thick sauce.

Add the chicken pieces and onion to the remaining lard in the frying pan and cook over a medium heat, turning frequently, until the chicken is lightly browned and the onion is softened – you may need to add extra lard.

Stir in the sauce and heat until bubbling. Reduce the heat, cover and simmer gently for 20–30 minutes, or until the chicken is cooked through and tender. Add a little more water if the sauce dries out.

Serve warm rather than piping hot.

# Black beans with shredded greens

## *Feijao preto*

### Serves 6–8

1 kg/2 lb 4 oz black beans

1 red onion, roughly chopped

2 tbsp olive oil

1 green cabbage, about
1 kg/2 lb 4 oz

2 tbsp water

salt and pepper or chilli flakes

### To serve

125 g/4 1/2 oz farofa (toasted manioc
flour or Indian gari) or Brazil nuts,
roughly crushed and toasted in a
dry frying pan

Piri-piri, Tabasco sauce or other
hot sauce

about 250 g/9 oz feta-type crumbly
salty white cheese, crumbled
(optional)

hard-boiled eggs, quartered (allow
1 per person; optional)

Suitable for vegetarians, this is a balanced dish of beans and fresh greens, eaten with assorted fiery little salsas. It is the everyday version of the Saturday *feijoada*, Brazil's national dish – a stupendous feast which takes three days to prepare.

Check over the beans and remove any tiny stones. You can presoak the beans in cold water overnight to speed up the cooking process, but this is not essential.

Drain the beans, if necessary, and put in an earthenware pot or enamel casserole with the onion and oil. Pour in enough hot water to cover the beans generously – allow at least 3 fingers' width of water above the surface of the beans. Do not add salt. Bring to the boil, then reduce the heat to low. Cover tightly and simmer for 2 hours (3 hours if the beans were very dry), or until completely tender and the skins are soft, checking regularly and adding more boiling water if necessary. Alternatively, transfer the pot to a preheated oven at 160°C/325°F/Gas Mark 3, or use a pressure cooker – very popular with bean cooks – and cook for 40 minutes.

Meanwhile, trim the cabbage sparingly – remove any discoloured outer leaves but leave as much of the dark green as possible. Halve the cabbage and cut out the core. Use a very sharp knife or a food processor to shred the leaves as finely as you can. Pack the shredded leaves into a large saucepan, add the water and bring to the boil. Cover tightly, give the saucepan a shake and cook for 2–3 minutes, or until the cabbage softens slightly but retains its texture. Drain well.

Increase the heat under the beans or transfer the pot to the hob over a high heat and cook to evaporate the excess water – they should not be the consistency of soup. Season to taste with salt and pepper or chilli flakes.

Serve the beans in deep bowls, with the shredded cabbage and farofa and Piri-piri. Serve the crumbled cheese and hard-boiled egg quarters separately, if using, for people to add if they please.

# Sweet-sour braised pork

## *Pibil de carne de cerdo*

**Serves 4–6**

1 pork joint, weighing 2 kg/
4 lb 8 oz, on the bone
(shoulder is good)

300 ml/10 fl oz white wine vinegar

6 garlic cloves, roughly crushed

1 tsp peppercorns, roughly crushed

1 tsp allspice berries, roughly
crushed

1 tsp salt

2 red peppers or 75 g/2¾ oz dried
ancho chilli (mild and fruity)

2–3 fresh red chillies or 75 g/2¾ oz
dried guajillo chillies (sharp and hot)

2–3 tbsp boiling water (optional)

1 banana leaf, central vein removed
(optional)

2–3 fresh or dried thyme sprigs

2 tbsp green olives

plain white rice, to serve

### Relish

3–4 mild red onions, finely sliced

juice and finely grated rind of 1 lime

1 tsp salt

2 tbsp chopped fresh coriander
leaves

This dish takes its name from the *pib*, a pit barbecue or earth oven still in use in the Yucatan. Gentle cooking in a closed pot ensures that the meat is tender. Wrapping the meat in a banana leaf gives it added flavour and gloriously sticky juices.

Wipe the pork joint. Slash the skin in several places with a sharp knife without cutting through to the meat and put in a large non-reactive bowl.

Put the vinegar, garlic, peppercorns, allspice and salt in a blender or food processor and blend thoroughly. Pour the mixture over the meat, cover and leave to marinate in the refrigerator for 2 hours.

Meanwhile, if using fresh red peppers and chillies, deseed and dice. If using dried chillies, remove and discard the seeds and soak the flesh in the boiling water for 20 minutes or so to soften the flesh.

Preheat the oven to 150°C/300°F/Gas Mark 2. Drain the joint, reserving the marinade. Put the marinade in the blender or food processor with the fresh peppers and chillies or dried chillies and their soaking water and blend to a smooth paste. Spread the paste over the meat and wrap in the banana leaf, if you have one, securing the parcel with uncoloured string. Put the meat in a heavy-based casserole or earthenware pot into which it just fits. Tuck in the thyme sprigs and olives and add enough water to come halfway up the meat. Cover tightly.

Cook in the preheated oven for 2–3 hours, or until the meat is tender but not yet falling apart. Uncover, increase the oven temperature to 190°C/375°F/Gas Mark 5 and cook for a further 20 minutes, or until the skin is browned and the juices have reduced to a sticky sauce.

Meanwhile, prepare the relish. Toss the onions with the lime juice and salt in a non-reactive bowl. Cover and leave to marinate at room temperature. Add the lime rind and coriander.

Remove the banana leaf, then cut the meat into thick slices and serve with the onion relish and a steaming heap of plain white rice.

# Baked beans with sweetcorn topping

## *Pastel de frijoles pintos con choclo*

**Serves 4–6**

6 tbsp olive oil or butter

750 g/1 lb 10 oz onions,
finely sliced

3–4 garlic cloves, finely chopped

1 tsp cumin seeds

1 tsp fresh or dried oregano leaves

500 g/1 lb 2 oz fresh tomatoes,
peeled and chopped, or canned
chopped tomatoes

500 g/1 lb 2 oz pumpkin, peeled,
deseeded and cut into small dice

750 g/1 lb 10 oz cooked pinto or
borlotti beans, drained

2 tbsp green olives, stoned
and chopped

2 tbsp raisins

1 tbsp icing sugar

1 tsp dried chilli flakes

salt and pepper

*Topping*

1.3 kg/3 lb fresh or frozen
sweetcorn kernels

375 ml/13 fl oz milk

1 egg, beaten

Red beans in a spicy tomato sauce are baked under a crisp topping of puréed sweetcorn in this vegetarian recipe from the Chilean highlands.

Heat 4 tablespoons of the oil in a heavy-based saucepan, add the onions and garlic and cook over a very low heat, stirring occasionally, for 20–30 minutes, or until the onions are soft and golden but not browned.

Add the cumin seeds, oregano and tomatoes and heat until bubbling, mashing the tomatoes down with a potato masher, for 10 minutes, or until you have a thick, sticky sauce.

Add the pumpkin and heat until bubbling. Reduce the heat to low, cover and cook for a further 10–15 minutes, or until the pumpkin is softened but not collapsed. Stir in the beans, olives and raisins. Reheat gently and simmer for 5 minutes to marry the flavours. Season to taste with salt and pepper.

Meanwhile, preheat the oven to 180°C/350°F/ Gas Mark 4. Put the sweetcorn kernels in a blender or food processor with the milk and blend to a purée. Transfer to a saucepan and cook, stirring constantly, for 5 minutes, or until the mixture has thickened slightly. Remove from the heat and leave to cool to finger heat. Stir in the egg and season to taste with salt and pepper.

Spread the bean mixture in an earthenware gratin dish (or use individual baking dishes) and top with a thick layer of the sweetcorn mixture – the bean base and the topping should be of roughly equal thickness. Drizzle with the remaining oil or dot small pieces of butter over the surface and sprinkle with the sugar and chilli flakes.

Bake in the preheated oven for 30 minutes, or until browned and bubbling. Serve hot.

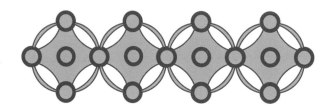

# Chicken with chilli and chocolate

## *Pollo en mole*

**Serves 6–8**

1 whole garlic bulb

1 chicken, weighing 2 kg/4 lb 8 oz

4 fresh mint sprigs

1/2 tsp black peppercorns

2–3 cloves

salt

*Sauce*

3–4 tbsp olive oil (lard is traditional)

1 large onion, finely sliced

1 ripe plantain or unripe banana

1 red pepper, deseeded and diced

500 g/1 lb 2 oz fresh or canned tomatoes, peeled and chopped

100 g/3 1/2 oz blanched almonds or peanuts, toasted and crushed

1 tsp cumin seeds

1 tsp allspice berries

1 soft cornmeal tortilla, torn into pieces, or 1 tbsp tortilla chips

50 g/1 3/4 oz dried chillies, deseeded, soaked in boiling water for 20 minutes and drained

2 tbsp raisins

finely grated rind of 1 orange

2 tbsp cocoa powder or 50 g/ 1 3/4 oz high-quality plain chocolate

*To serve*

warm cornmeal tortillas

Guacamole (see page 296)

In this classic Mexican party dish, gently poached chicken pieces are finished in a mole (pronounced *moll-ay*), a spicy chilli sauce flavoured with cocoa powder, which takes its name from the mortar in which the flavourings are crushed.

Score round the centre of the garlic bulb. Cut the chicken into 12 neat pieces, rinse and put in a large saucepan with enough cold water to cover generously – about 1.5 litres/2 3/4 pints. Bring to the boil, skimming off the foam, then add the garlic, mint sprigs, peppercorns, cloves and a little salt. Return to the boil, then reduce the heat, cover and simmer gently for 30–40 minutes, or until the chicken is tender. Remove the chicken pieces and set aside. When cool enough to handle, remove the skin, if you like. Strain the stock and reserve.

Meanwhile, for the sauce, heat 2 tablespoons of the oil in a large frying pan, add the onion and cook over a low heat, stirring occasionally, for 10–15 minutes, or until soft and golden. Remove with a slotted spoon and set aside. Peel the plantain and cut into chunks. Reheat the oily juices in the pan, add the red pepper and cook for 5–6 minutes, or until softened but not browned. Add the tomatoes and plantain and heat until bubbling, then reduce the heat, cover and cook over a low heat for 20 minutes, or until the plantain is tender.

Heat a dry frying pan over a medium–high heat, add the nuts and spices and cook, shaking frequently, for 3–4 minutes, or until toasted, being careful not to burn them. Transfer to a food processor and pulse briefly. Set aside.

Tip the onions and the tomato mixture into a blender or food processor. Add the tortilla and chillies and their soaking water and blend until smooth – you may need to add a little of the reserved chicken stock.

Add the remaining oil to the large frying pan and reheat. Add the crushed nuts and spices and cook, stirring, for 1–2 minutes, to develop the flavours. Add the tomato mixture and heat until bubbling, then reduce the heat and cook gently for 5 minutes. Add the raisins, orange rind and 1 litre/1 3/4 pints of the reserved chicken stock. Bring to the boil, then reduce the heat and simmer gently for 20 minutes, or until the sauce thickens and the liquid is reduced by a third. Meanwhile, preheat the oven to 180°C/350°F/Gas Mark 4.

Stir the cocoa powder into the sauce and heat gently without boiling.

Pour the sauce over the chicken in an ovenproof dish, cover with foil and cook in the preheated oven for 20–25 minutes. Serve with warm tortillas and Guacamole.

# Bean casserole with potatoes, sweetcorn and pumpkin

## *Cocido limeño*

**Serves 4–6**

250 g/9 oz butter beans

500 g/1 lb 2 oz yellow-fleshed potatoes, peeled and cubed

500 g/1 lb 2 oz pumpkin or butternut squash, deseeded and cubed

500 g/1 lb 2 oz fresh or frozen sweetcorn kernels

salt and pepper

*Flavouring salsa*

2–3 yellow or red chillies, deseeded and chopped

1 small onion, finely chopped

6 spring onions, green parts included, finely chopped

2–3 garlic cloves, finely chopped

2 tbsp olive oil

*To serve*

2 tbsp fresh basil leaves, chopped

2 tbsp crumbled feta-type crumbly salty white cheese

This dish is made with the plump, creamy new season lima or butter beans, which appear in Peruvian markets just before Christmas. Satisfying and delicious, it does not include meat and is traditionally served at the fasting supper of Christmas Eve.

Soak the beans in cold water overnight. Drain and transfer to a large saucepan with enough water to cover by 2 fingers' width. Do not add salt. Bring to the boil, then reduce the heat and simmer very gently for 1½–2 hours, or until the beans are tender.

Meanwhile, put all the salsa ingredients in a small saucepan and cook over a medium heat, stirring frequently, for 5 minutes, to marry the flavours. Set aside.

When the beans are tender, add the potatoes and pumpkin and top up with enough boiling water to submerge all the ingredients. Return to the boil, then reduce the heat, cover and cook gently for 20–30 minutes, or until the vegetables are tender. Season to taste.

Stir in the sweetcorn kernels and reheat until bubbling. Stir in the salsa and cook for a further 10 minutes to marry the flavours and reduce the cooking juices. The dish should be juicy but not soupy. Sprinkle with the chopped basil and crumbled cheese and serve immediately.

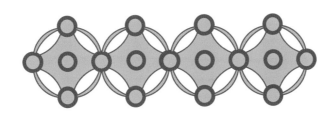

# Chicken with prawns, cashew nuts and coconut

## Ximxim de galinha

**Serves 4–6**

1 chicken, weighing 2 kg/4 lb 8 oz, cut into 12 neat pieces

450 g/1 lb fresh tomatoes, peeled and diced, or canned chopped tomatoes

1 onion, finely sliced

2–3 fresh mint sprigs

450 g/1 lb raw peeled prawns or large shrimps

300 ml/10 fl oz canned coconut milk

sea salt

*Vatapa salsa*

100 g/3½ oz dried shrimps or 175 g/6 oz small cooked peeled shrimps

100 g/3½ oz toasted cashew nuts and/or peanuts

1 onion, roughly chopped

1 heaped tbsp grated fresh ginger

4 tbsp dende oil or olive oil and a pinch of ground saffron or turmeric

*To serve*

lime quarters

Piri-piri or Tabasco sauce

plain white rice

From Brazil, this one-stop dish features *vatapa*, a bread-thickened dipping sauce usually made with the semi-dried shrimp of Bahia and eaten in much the same way as a mayonnaise, used to thicken the cooking juices.

Wipe over the chicken pieces and put in a large saucepan with the tomatoes, onion, mint sprigs and enough water to cover. Bring to the boil, then reduce the heat, cover loosely and simmer for 20–30 minutes, or until the chicken is cooked through but not yet tender. Remove the mint sprigs. Remove the chicken joints, and when cool enough to handle, remove the skin. Set aside.

Reheat the tomato mixture until bubbling and cook for 6–8 minutes, or until reduced to a jammy sauce. Add the prawns, bubble up again and cook for 1–2 minutes, or until the prawns are pink. Remove from the heat.

Meanwhile, make the salsa. Put the dried shrimps and nuts in a food processor and process briefly. Add the onion and ginger and process again till reduced to a thick paste.

Heat the oil in a large frying pan, add the paste and cook over a medium heat, stirring, for 2–3 minutes, or until the onion is slightly softened and a fragrant steam rises. Add the chicken pieces, turning until thoroughly coated with the paste. Pour in enough water to come halfway up the chicken pieces and bring to the boil. Reduce the heat and season with a little salt. Cover loosely and simmer gently for 10 minutes, or until the chicken is tender and the flavours are well blended.

Combine the tomato and prawn mixture with the chicken mixture, stir in the coconut milk and reheat gently. Check the seasoning. Serve with lime quarters, Piri-piri and plain white rice.

# Pot-roast beef with Guatemalan rice

## Carne en jocon con arroz guatemalteco

Serves 4–6

1.5 kg/3 lb 5 oz boned stewing beef, tied in a single piece

4 tbsp olive oil

4 garlic cloves, peeled but kept whole

2 large onions, finely chopped

500 g/1 lb 2 oz carrots, scraped and cut into chunks

2 fresh green or dried red chillies, deseeded and chopped

1 tsp crumbled dried oregano

500 g/1 lb 2 oz fresh red tomatoes, peeled, deseeded and roughly chopped, or canned chopped tomatoes

500 g/1 lb 2 oz fresh tomatillos, husks removed and chopped, or canned tomatillos

1 tbsp chopped fresh coriander leaves, to garnish

salt and pepper

### Guatemalan rice

4 tbsp olive oil

500 g/1 lb 2 oz white long-grain rice

2 garlic cloves, chopped

1 tbsp diced celery

1 tbsp diced green pepper

2 tbsp diced tomato

handful of fresh or frozen peas

Guatemala's succulent beef casserole is made with *tomatillos*, which resemble green tomatoes, although they are actually part of the physalis family. If you can't find tomatillos, use ordinary tomatoes and include the grated rind and juice of a lemon.

Wipe the stewing beef and season to taste with salt and pepper.

Heat the oil in a large flameproof casserole into which the joint fits comfortably, add the garlic cloves, onions and carrots and cook over a medium heat, stirring frequently, until lightly coloured. Remove with a slotted spoon, draining the oil back into the casserole, and set aside. Add the meat and cook, turning frequently, until browned on all sides. Add the chillies and oregano and cook, stirring, for a further minute.

Add the tomatoes and tomatillos and enough water to come three-quarters of the way up the meat. Return the reserved garlic, onion and carrot mixture to the casserole. Season to taste with salt and pepper and bring to the boil. Reduce the heat, cover tightly, using a piece of foil as well as the lid, and simmer very gently for 1$^{1}$/$_{2}$–2 hours, or until the meat is perfectly tender. Alternatively, transfer the casserole to

a preheated oven at 150°C/300°F/Gas Mark 2. You shouldn't need to add extra liquid, but if you do, add the bare minimum and make sure that it is boiling.

Meanwhile, make the rice. Heat the oil in a large frying pan, add the rice, garlic, celery and green pepper and cook over a medium heat, stirring, for 3–4 minutes, or until the rice grains turn transparent. Add the tomato and enough water to cover by a finger-width's depth. Bring to the boil and season to taste with salt and pepper, then reduce the heat and cook gently for 15–20 minutes, or until the grains are just tender. Stir in the peas and cook for a further 2–3 minutes.

When the meat is perfectly tender and the juices reduced to a sticky sauce, transfer the meat to a warmed serving dish and leave to rest for 10 minutes. Cut into thick slices and serve with the cooking juices, scattered with the coriander. Serve with the rice.

# Braised lamb with garlic and orange

## *Seco de carnero*

### Serves 4–6

1 boned, rolled shoulder of
lamb, weighing 1.5–2 kg/
3 lb 5 oz–4 lb 8 oz

12–18 garlic cloves, unpeeled

finely grated rind and juice of
2 bitter oranges or 1 lemon and
1 sweet orange

1/2 tsp allspice berries, crushed

short length of cinnamon stick,
roughly crushed

150 ml/5 fl oz dry white wine

large handful of fresh coriander
leaves

2 green chillies, deseeded and
roughly chopped

salt and pepper

### To serve

cooked corn on the cob, chopped
into thick slices

cooked butternut squash, peeled
and cut into chunks

This is a Peruvian method of cooking a shoulder of lamb or kid, which benefits from slow, lengthy cooking to soften the meat and tame the garlic, melting it into a delicious, gentle sauce.

Wipe the meat and season to taste with salt and pepper. Put into a flameproof casserole into which it just fits neatly. Pack the garlic cloves around the side. Scatter over the orange rind, allspice and cinnamon and drizzle with the orange juice. Add the wine and enough water to come halfway up the meat. Bring to the boil, then reduce the heat, cover tightly, using a piece of foil as well as the lid, and simmer very gently for 1 1/2–2 hours, or until the meat is perfectly tender. Alternatively, transfer the casserole to a preheated oven at 150°C/300°F/Gas Mark 2. Check every now and again, adding a little boiling water if the juices are drying out.

Transfer the meat to a warmed serving dish. Squeeze the garlic flesh from the skins into a blender or food processor, add the coriander, chillies and cooking juices and blend to a purée. Return to the casserole and reheat gently, diluting with boiling water if necessary.

Carve the lamb into thick slices and serve with corn on the cob, butternut squash and the sauce.

# Vegetable Dishes and Salads

In pre-Columbian traditions as well as the Hispanic kitchen, vegetables are treated as dishes in their own right rather than as side dishes. Since vegetables are served as a separate course or the centrepiece of a light meal, attention is paid to nutritional balance.

Where there is no meat or fish, protein is often included in the form of nuts or dairy products together with a starch food by way of accompaniment. Depending on the region, this might be cornmeal tortillas, *arepas* (thick tortillas made with white cornmeal), *patacones* (plantain chips) or chunks of fresh corn cobs. And in rural areas and regions where wheat is a luxury, root vegetables take the place of bread.

# Guacamole with plantain chips

## Guacamole con patacones

Serves 4–6

2–3 ripe avocados (depending on size)

2 green chillies, preferably serrano, deseeded and chopped

1 small onion, roughly chopped

1 tbsp chopped fresh coriander

1 tsp sea salt

1 large tomato, peeled, deseeded and diced

lime juice, for dressing (optional)

### Plantain chips

2 firm plantains or unripe bananas

vegetable oil, for frying

salt

In Mexico and Central America, the avocado's place of origin, a guacamole is never a smooth purée – it is lumpy, with all elements visible. Here it is teamed with plantain chips, *patacones* or *tostones*, a popular snack in the banana-growing regions.

For the plantain chips, slice the plantains as thick as your thumb, then drop into salted water and leave to soak for 30 minutes, or until you can push the flesh out of the skins. Drain and pat dry.

Meanwhile, halve the avocados lengthways, remove the stones, reserving one, and scoop the flesh into a bowl. Roughly chop with a knife.

Put the chillies, onion, coriander and salt in a blender or food processor and blend to a purée.

Fold the purée into the avocados in the bowl, then stir in the tomato. Insert the reserved avocado stone in the centre of the mixture to slow down the inevitable browning – it sounds odd but it seems to work! If you prepare the guacamole well ahead of serving, dress it with lime juice as an added precaution against browning – this changes the delicate balance of flavour, but some people like the touch of sharpness.

Over a medium–high heat, heat enough oil to submerge the plantain slices in a large frying pan – they need plenty of room. Wait until a faint blue haze rises from the oil. Add the slices, in small batches, and cook over a medium heat for 4–5 minutes, or until fairly soft but not yet crisp. Remove and drain on kitchen paper in a single layer. Sandwich the slices between 2 sheets of clingfilm. Using a small chopping board or rolling pin, flatten the slices until reduced to half their thickness (you can buy a special little wooden press that performs this task quickly and easily).

Reheat the oil to 180–190°C/350–375°F, or until a cube of bread browns in 30 seconds. Add the flattened slices, in small batches, to the oil and cook for 2–3 minutes, or until brown and crisp on the outside and still meltingly soft on the inside. Remove and drain on kitchen paper.

Serve the guacamole as a dip with the hot plantain chips.

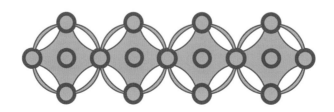

# Gratin of green chillies with cream and cheese

## *Rajas poblanas*

**Serves 4–6**

750 g/1 lb 10 oz thin-fleshed, mild green chillies, preferably Anaheim

250 ml/9 fl oz single cream

250 ml/9 fl oz double cream

250 g/9 oz feta-type crumbly salty white cheese, crumbled

salt and pepper

soft cornmeal tortillas, to serve

This is an everyday dish that everyone knows how to cook and no one bothers with a recipe for. The utterly delicious combination of peppery, lemony chillies and sweet, rich cream offers the perfect balance of texture and flavour.

Wipe the chillies, but don't remove the stalks or seeds. Using tongs, hold the chillies over a gas flame, or cook under a preheated grill or oven on the highest setting, until the skins are black and blistered in places. Transfer to a polythene or paper bag and leave to stand for 10 minutes to loosen the skins. Remove the skins. Slice the flesh into ribbons (rajas) and arrange in a gratin dish.

Meanwhile, heat all the cream in a small saucepan and remove it as soon as it reaches boiling point. Pour over the chilli ribbons and sprinkle with the cheese. Season with a little salt and pepper – not too much, as the cheese is already salty and one or two of the chillies may be fiery.

Preheat the grill to very high. Cook the chillies for 8–10 minutes, or until brown and bubbling. Meanwhile, wrap the tortillas in foil and warm through in a preheated low oven for 5 minutes. Serve the gratin piping hot with the warmed tortillas for mopping up.

# Baked sweet potato with garlic salsa

## *Batata con mojo*

Serves 4–6

1 kg/2 lb 4 oz sweet potatoes

2 tbsp chopped fresh coriander, to garnish

### *Mojo dressing*

2 tbsp olive oil

4 garlic cloves, crushed

juice of 3–4 oranges (about 150 ml/5 fl oz)

juice and grated rind of 1 lemon

1/2 tsp sea salt

This simple country dish is popular in Cuba. Ring the changes with plantain, cassava, pumpkin, potatoes or any plain-cooked vegetables.

Preheat the oven to 180°C/350°F/Gas Mark 4.

Wash the sweet potatoes and pat dry. Bake in the preheated oven for 40 minutes, then test for softness with a knife – they may take up to a further 20 minutes to cook, depending on their variety and shape.

Meanwhile, make the dressing. Heat the oil and garlic in a small saucepan, add the citrus juices, lemon rind and salt and leave to bubble for 3–4 minutes, or until blended.

When the sweet potatoes are perfectly tender, remove from the oven. When cool enough to handle, remove the skins and dice the flesh into bite-sized pieces.

Fold the diced sweet potato into the dressing. Serve at room temperature with the chopped coriander sprinkled over.

# New potatoes with tomato, cheese and eggs

## *Pipián*

**Serves 4–6**

1 kg/2 lb 4 oz small new yellow-fleshed potatoes, scrubbed

2–3 hard-boiled eggs, peeled

25 g/1 oz butter

1 onion, finely chopped

500 g/1 lb 2 oz tomatoes, peeled, deseeded and diced, or 3 tbsp passata

150 ml/5 fl oz double cream

150 g/5¹/₂ oz mild Cheddar-type cheese, grated

salt

*To serve*

2 tbsp roasted unsalted peanuts, roughly crushed

1 tsp dried chilli flakes

Here, a creamy cheese and tomato sauce is poured over potatoes and eggs, with a sprinkling of crushed peanuts. In Peru, where this dish originates, it is made with *papas criollas*, nutty little yellow-fleshed potatoes that can be eaten in a single bite.

Cook the potatoes in their skins in a large saucepan of salted water for 15–20 minutes, or until tender. Drain the potatoes thoroughly and transfer to a warmed serving dish. Cut the hard-boiled eggs into quarters and arrange them among the potatoes.

Meanwhile, heat the butter in a large frying pan. As soon as it is foaming, add the onion and cook over a low heat, stirring frequently, for 10 minutes, or until soft and golden. Add the tomatoes and heat until bubbling, mashing to blend. Cook, stirring, for a further 5 minutes.

Stir in the cream, bubble up again and add the cheese. Continue to cook, stirring, until the cheese melts and the sauce is pink and smooth. Taste and add salt if necessary.

Pour the sauce over the potatoes and eggs, sprinkle with the peanuts and chilli flakes and serve immediately.

# Prawn salad with chicken and palm hearts

## Salata de palmito, frango e camarón

Serves 4–6

450 g/1 lb fresh or canned palm hearts

150 g/5¹/₂ oz cooked peeled prawns

150 g/5¹/₂ oz cooked chicken breast, shredded

1 small cos lettuce, shredded

1 tbsp fresh or toasted finely shredded coconut

### Dressing

6 tbsp olive oil

2 tbsp lime or lemon juice

few drops of Piri-piri or Tabasco sauce

1 tsp sea salt

This simple salad is popular in Brazil, where the edible palm is widely cultivated as a crop. If palm hearts are unavailable either canned or fresh, substitute kohlrabi, cut into matchsticks, or shredded white cabbage – texture matters as much as flavour.

Beat the dressing ingredients together in a non-reactive bowl.

If the palm hearts are fresh, trim off any remnants of the fibrous exterior and use the slicing device on a box grater to give you long, thin ribbons like tagliatelle. If canned, drain and thinly slice in the same way.

Combine the palm hearts with the dressing in the bowl, cover and leave to marinate at room temperature for 1–2 hours.

Add the prawns and chicken to the bowl and toss to combine. Heap onto a bed of shredded lettuce, then sprinkle with the coconut.

# Quinoa and sweetcorn paella with mint

## *Picada de quinua*

**Serves 4–6**

450 g/1 lb quinoa

2 tbsp olive oil

2–3 garlic cloves, chopped

2 red or yellow chillies (preferably native to the Andes), deseeded and finely chopped

1 large tomato, peeled, deseeded and diced

2 tbsp fresh or frozen sweetcorn kernels

1 tbsp fresh mint leaves

salt (optional)

cos lettuce leaves, to serve

Quinoa (pronounced *keenwa*) is a highly nutritious grain native to the Amazonian highlands. This nutty little seed has a semi-transparent shell that pops when cooked. The leaves are also edible and make an excellent substitute for spinach.

Put the quinoa in a sieve and rinse under cold running water until the water runs clear.

Transfer the quinoa to a large saucepan and cover with double its own volume of water. Bring to the boil, then reduce the heat and simmer for 20 minutes, or until the grains have popped their shells – they will look translucent with little white curls – and have absorbed all the water.

Meanwhile, heat the oil in a large frying pan, add the garlic and chilli and cook over a medium heat, stirring, for 2–3 minutes, or until the garlic is softened. Stir in the tomato and sweetcorn, heat until bubbling and bubble for 1 minute.

Stir in the cooked quinoa and reheat gently to marry the flavours. Taste and add salt if necessary. Chop the mint leaves and stir into the mixture.

Serve with crisp cos lettuce leaves for scooping. Paella is traditionally eaten from the circular pan in which it is cooked, each person eating the portion directly in front of them.

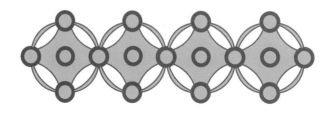

# Sweet and sour pumpkin

## Hogao de auyama

Serves 4–6

1 kg/2 lb 4 oz pumpkin

4 tbsp olive oil

1 large onion, finely sliced

1–2 hot red chillies, deseeded and finely chopped

1 kg/2 lb 4 oz fresh ripe tomatoes, peeled and diced, or canned chopped tomatoes

1 tbsp sultanas

2 tbsp red wine vinegar

finely grated rind and juice of 1 bitter orange or lemon

salt

Plantain Chips, to serve (see page 296)

*Hogao*, a slow-cooked onion and tomato sauce, is the basic flavouring of Colombia's criollo kitchen. Chunks of sweet pumpkin are added to the thick, jammy sauce in this recipe, which is sharpened with vinegar and sweetened with sultanas.

Peel, deseed and dice the pumpkin – you will need a very sharp knife.

Heat the oil in a large saucepan, add the onion and cook over a very low heat, stirring occasionally, for at least 15 minutes, or until soft and golden but not browned. Add the chillies and tomatoes and heat until bubbling. Reduce the heat and simmer for 20–30 minutes, or until all the ingredients reduce to a jammy sauce.

Stir in the pumpkin, sultanas, vinegar and orange rind and juice. Bubble up again, then reduce the heat and cook, loosely covered, for 20 minutes, or until the flavours are well blended and the pumpkin is perfectly tender.

Serve at room temperature with crisp Plantain Chips.

# Corn on the cob with two salsas

## *Maiz tierno asado con dos salsas*

**Serves 4–6**

8–12 corn on the cob in their husks

*Chimichurri*

1 small mild red onion, diced

4 garlic cloves, finely chopped

4 tbsp finely chopped fresh
flat-leaf parsley

1 tsp fresh thyme leaves

finely grated rind and juice of
2 lemons

250 ml/9 fl oz olive oil

*Piri-piri*

100 g/3¹/₂ oz hot red chillies,
preferably malagueta

100 g/3¹/₂ oz red peppers

100 ml/3¹/₂ fl oz white wine vinegar

1 tsp sea salt

Corn cobs left in their husks – nature's wrapper – taste all the better when allowed to cook in their own steam. They are ideal served with a couple of dipping salsas – a mild *chimichurri* and a fiery *piri-piri*.

First make the salsas. Pack all the ingredients for the chimichurri into a screw-top jar. Screw on the lid, shake and then leave to infuse at room temperature for 1–2 hours, or overnight in the refrigerator.

To make the piri-piri, remove the stalks from the chillies (rinse your fingers after handling them and don't rub your eyes). Deseed and roughly chop the red peppers. Heat the vinegar with an equal quantity of water and the salt in a small saucepan over a medium heat, stirring until the salt has dissolved. Pour the hot vinegar into a blender or food processor, add the chillies and red pepper and blend to a purée. Leave to cool – it is ready to serve as soon as it has cooled.

Pull off the silky tassel at the top of each corn cob, keeping the leaves intact. Light a barbecue, preheat a grill to medium–high or preheat the oven to 200°C/400°F/Gas Mark 6.

Cook the corn cobs on the barbecue, under the preheated grill or in the preheated oven, turning frequently, for 8–12 minutes. If cooking on the barbecue or under the grill, sprinkle the husks with water from your fingers if they start to blacken.

Serve the corn cobs in their husks, with the salsas separately. Encourage your guests to chop the cobs into thick slices for dipping into the salsas.

# Plantain and aubergine ratatouille

## *Boronia de platano*

### Serves 4–6

500 g/1 lb 2 oz ripe plantains or unripe bananas, sliced

500 g/1 lb 2 oz firm aubergines, diced

4–5 tbsp olive oil

2 shallots or red onions, finely sliced

2 large carrots, scraped and diced

1–2 celery sticks, chopped

2 garlic cloves, roughly chopped

2–3 dried chillies, deseeded and torn

1 tsp cumin seeds

salt and pepper

### To serve

1 tbsp fresh basil leaves, roughly torn

150 g/5½ oz feta-type crumbly salty white cheese, crumbled (optional)

Prepared in a similar way to a Provençal ratatouille, this dish consists of a combination of vegetables that complement each other, flavoured with chilli and cumin. The vegetables should be more or less matched in size and shape.

Soak the plantains in a bowl of salted water for 10 minutes to loosen the skins. Push the plantain flesh out of the skins. Cook in a saucepan of lightly salted boiling water for 20–25 minutes, or until tender but not mushy. Drain and reserve.

Meanwhile, put the aubergine in a colander, sprinkle with salt and leave the juices to drain.

Heat the oil in a heavy-based flameproof casserole, add the shallots and cook over a very low heat, stirring occasionally, for at least 20 minutes, or until soft and golden but not browned. Remove with a slotted spoon, draining the oil back into the casserole, and set aside. Add the carrots and celery and cook over a medium heat, stirring occasionally, for about 10 minutes, or until softened. Remove with a slotted spoon and set aside.

Rinse the aubergine under cold running water and pat dry. Reheat the casserole, add the garlic, aubergine, chillies and cumin seeds and cook over a medium heat, stirring frequently, for about 15 minutes, or until the aubergine softens and caramelizes slightly – you may need to add a little more oil. Stir in the plantain slices, shallots and carrot and celery, and turn everything in the oily juices.

Cook over a low heat, stirring, for a further 5 minutes to marry the flavours. Season to taste with salt and pepper.

Serve warm or cool – never chilled – scattered with the torn basil leaves and the crumbled cheese, if using.

# Desserts

Sweet dishes are relatively new to the region, since sugar was not known in the Americas until sugar cane plantations were established in the Caribbean in the colonial period. The taste-enhancer for fruit was (and still is) a dusting of fiery chilli, a seasoning used for at least 5,000 years. The only source of sweetness was wild-gathered honeycomb.

Plant foods native to the region include chocolate, an infusion made with the fermented sun-dried seeds of a forest tree, and vanilla, the seed pods of a white-flowered tree orchid. These home-grown flavourings quickly made their way into the pastries and custards that arrived in the New World as the speciality of Spanish and Portuguese nuns.

# Caramel pineapple custards

## *Flan de piña*

Serves 4–6

*Caramel*

3 tbsp caster sugar

3 tsp water

juice of ½ lemon

*Custard*

300 ml/10 fl oz pineapple juice

250 g/9 oz granulated sugar

6 large egg yolks (add an extra
2 if the eggs are small)

*To serve (optional)*

4–6 tbsp diced ripe pawpaw or
mango

1 tbsp fresh mint leaves

In this popular milk and egg dessert – Latin American children love it as much as children in Spain – the milk is replaced with the juice of a fresh pineapple, which is native to the Amazonian lowlands.

Preheat the oven to 180°C/350°F/Gas Mark 4.

Make the caramel. Using a wooden spoon, stir the caster sugar into the water and lemon juice in a heavy-based saucepan, bring to the boil over a high heat and cook for a few seconds, until the water evaporates completely and the sugar turns a rich golden brown. Remove from the heat, leave to cool briefly, then divide the caramel between 4–6 individual custard moulds or soufflé dishes. Roll it around to coat the bases. Set aside to cool.

To make the custard, put the pineapple juice and granulated sugar in a heavy-based saucepan and heat gently, stirring with a wooden spoon, until the sugar has dissolved. Increase the heat and boil steadily for 15 minutes, or until the volume has reduced by a third. It is ready when the syrup leaves a transparent trail when you lift the spoon.

Meanwhile, put the egg yolks in a blender or food processor and blend thoroughly or beat with a hand-held whisk until well blended. Add the hot syrup in a steady stream with the motor running or beat in vigorously with the whisk. Pour the mixture into the prepared mould or dishes. Transfer to a roasting tin and pour in enough water to come halfway up the sides. Cover with foil, shiny-side down.

Bake the custards in the preheated oven for 30–40 minutes, depending on the size of the moulds, or until set – they are ready when firm to the touch.

Leave to cool before unmoulding: run a knife around the side of the mould or dish, lay a plate over the top and invert both plate and mould. Serve with pawpaw or mango and mint, if you like – the gentle flavours complement the smoothness and sharpness of the pineapple.

# Passion fruit and rum granita

## *Granita de caipirinha de maracujá*

**Makes about 1.5 litres/2½ pints**

12 ripe passion fruit
350 g/12 oz unrefined cane sugar
about 1 litre/1¾ pints water
cachaça or white rum
maraschino cherries, to serve
(optional)

Brazil's famous rum cocktail, in its everyday form, is a potent mix of *cachaça* – sugar cane rum – and lime juice poured over ice. Here, as served at every fashionable cocktail party in Rio, it is made with fresh passion fruit juice.

To prepare the passion fruit juice, make a small hole in the leathery skin of each passion fruit and squeeze the seeds and surrounding jelly and juice into a sieve set over a bowl. Press the pulp firmly with a wooden spoon to extract all the liquid – you need about 250 ml/9 fl oz, do not use more – it is very strong).

Put the sugar with half the water in a heavy-based saucepan. Bring gently to the boil, stirring until the sugar has dissolved. Leave to cool, then stir in the passion fruit juice and dilute to taste with the remaining water.

Pour the mixture into a very well-scrubbed baking tray and freeze for 30 minutes. Scrape the firm outer parts into the soft centre and freeze again. Repeat every 30 minutes, or until firm enough to form a spoonable slush.

Spoon the slush into long, well-chilled glasses, add a measure of cachaça and serve with a straw. For maximum impact, add a maraschino cherry and a cocktail parasol.

To store the granita for up to 3 months, transfer to a lidded plastic freezerproof container. Remove from the freezer 20 minutes before you are ready to serve and scrape it again as soon as it softens.

# Tropical fruit salad with chilli syrup

## Dulce de frutas tropicales

Serves 4–6

1 ripe pawpaw, peeled, deseeded and diced

1 ripe mango, stoned and diced

1 small ripe pineapple, peeled, cored and diced

100 g/3½ oz unrefined cane sugar

250 ml/9 fl oz water

2–3 hot fresh or dried red chillies

2–3 fresh basil sprigs (optional), to decorate

Chilli is traditional with fruit, heightening its natural sweetness and stimulating the taste buds. Fresh fruit cut into chunks to order is Mexico's favourite street food, and it always comes with an offer of the chilli shaker as well as the sugar bowl.

Fold the prepared fruit together in a bowl and sprinkle with half the sugar.

Put the remaining sugar with the water in a small saucepan. Bring gently to the boil, stirring until the sugar has dissolved. Add the chillies, return to the boil and bubble for 5 minutes, or until the volume is reduced by a third. Remove from the heat and leave to infuse for 30 minutes.

Remove the chillies and pour the syrup over the fruit, folding gently to blend. Serve decorated with the basil sprigs, if you like, and a few slivers of the syrupy chilli.

# Cherimoya sorbet with coffee-toffee sauce

## Sorbete de chirimoya con dulce de cafe

**Serves 6–8**

1 kg/2 lb 4 oz ripe cherimoyas (custard apples)

juice of I lemon

125 g/4¹/₂ oz caster sugar

300 ml/10 fl oz water

*Coffee-toffee*

400 ml/14 fl oz canned sweetened condensed milk

350 ml/12 fl oz canned unsweetened evaporated milk

1 heaped tbsp instant coffee granules

*To serve (optional)*

about 6–8 small macaroons, roughly crushed

about 50 g/1³/₄ oz chocolate-coated coffee beans

Cherimoya, also known as custard apple, tastes somewhere between a banana and a pear. The pale flesh makes a smooth, delicate cream that freezes perfectly. Here it is served with *dulce de leche*, a toffee sauce.

Quarter, skin and deseed the custard apples – the hard black seeds are distributed throughout the flesh and must be discarded. Sprinkle with the lemon juice.

Put the sugar and water in a heavy-based saucepan. Bring gently to the boil, stirring until the sugar has dissolved, then continue to boil for 5 minutes. Leave to cool.

Put the custard apples in a blender or food processor with the sugar syrup and blend to a purée. Pour into an ice-making tray and freeze for 2 hours, or until solid. Scoop out and blend again in the blender or food processor. Return to the ice-making tray and refreeze for 1–2 hours, or until firm.

Meanwhile, make the sauce. Combine the two milks in a heavy-based saucepan and cook over a medium heat, stirring steadily, for 20–30 minutes, or until thick and lightly caramelized. Stir in the coffee, making sure that the granules have dissolved, remove from the heat and set aside. Reheat gently without boiling just before serving.

When you are ready to serve, add the macaroons, if using, to 6–8 pretty glasses, and spoon over the sorbet. Sprinkle with the chocolate-coated coffee beans, if using. Serve the warm sauce separately.

# Winter fruit compote

## *Mazamorra*

**Serves 4–6**

100 g/3½ oz raisins

100 g/3½ oz prunes

100 g/3½ oz dried apricots or figs

finely pared rind of 1 orange

125 g/4½ oz soft dark brown sugar

1 tsp allspice berries, roughly crushed

1 tsp chopped fresh ginger

1 finger-length piece cinnamon stick, broken

1 litre/1¾ pints water, plus 2 tbsp

1 small pineapple, peeled, cored and cut into chunks

1 level tbsp cornflour

*To serve*

seeds of 1 pomegranate

2 tbsp toasted cashew nuts or pecan nuts

This winter fruit salad is made with dried fruit and fresh pineapple, spiced with ginger, cinnamon and allspice and thickened with a little cornflour – delicious served warm with cream. *Mazamorra* is particularly popular in Peru.

Put the dried fruit in a large saucepan with the orange rind, sugar and the spices, tied in a scrap of clean muslin or cloth to make a spice bag. Add the 1 litre/1¾ pints water, stir and bring to the boil. Reduce the heat and simmer for 30 minutes, or until the fruit is soft and juicy and the cooking juices are reduced by half. You may need to add more boiling water. Remove the spice bag and the orange rind, if you can find it.

Add the pineapple to the compote and reheat until just below boiling point. Simmer gently for 5 minutes to soften the pineapple and marry the flavours.

Meanwhile, blend the cornflour with the 2 tablespoons water to a smooth paste.

Stir the cornflour paste into the compote juices and heat gently, stirring constantly to avoid lumps, until the juices thicken. Remove from the heat and leave to cool slightly.

Transfer the compote to a glass serving dish, sprinkle with the pomegranate seeds and toasted nuts and serve.

# Pawpaw honeycomb mousse

## *Baba de lechosa*

Serves 4–6

1 ripe pawpaw, about 500 g/
1 lb 2 oz

juice and finely pared strips of rind
of 2 limes or small lemons

100 ml/3½ fl oz cold water,
plus 2 tbsp

2 sheets clear gelatine or 1 tbsp
powdered gelatine

300 ml/10 fl oz canned
unsweetened condensed milk or
fresh cream

3 egg whites

6 tbsp caster sugar

few fresh basil sprigs, to decorate
(optional)

crisp wafers or plain chocolate
fingers, to serve (optional)

The pawpaw, a tropical fruit native to Brazil, Mexico and the Caribbean, has a peach-strawberry-banana flavour that benefits from the sharpness of citrus juice – lime, lemon or bitter orange (the latter the regional favourite when in season).

Halve the pawpaw and remove the seeds in their gooey juice (reserve for decorating, if you like), scoop out the flesh and put in a blender or food processor with the lime juice. Blend to a purée.

Put the 100 ml/3½ fl oz water in a small saucepan and sprinkle with the gelatine (if using leaf gelatine, tear it into small pieces first). Leave for 10 minutes, or until the gelatine softens and becomes spongy, or follow the packet instructions. Set the saucepan over a low heat, stirring until the gelatine is dissolved – there is no need to bring it to the boil. Fold in the pawpaw purée and the condensed milk.

Whisk the egg whites in a bowl until stiff – be careful you don't over-whisk or they will become grainy. Add 4 tablespoons of the sugar, one spoonful at a time, and continue to whisk until you have a soft meringue. Fold the meringue into the pawpaw purée. Spoon into a soufflé dish or divide between 4–6 individual soufflé dishes, cover and chill in the refrigerator for 2–3 hours until set.

Put the remaining sugar in a small saucepan with the 2 tablespoons water and stir over a low heat until the sugar has dissolved. Add the lime rind, reserving some to decorate, and heat until bubbling, then reduce the heat and cook gently for 10 minutes, or until the water has all evaporated and the lime rind is tender.

Decorate the mousse with the reserved lime rind and basil sprigs, if using, just before serving. Serve with crisp little wafers or plain chocolate fingers, if you like. The reserved seeds can be crushed and used as a finishing sprinkle – the flavour is nutty and mustardy.

# Guava creams with vanilla

## *Dulce de guayaba con vainilla*

Serves 4–6

2–3 ripe guavas, about 450 g/1 lb total weight, cored, peeled and cut into chunks

2–3 ripe bananas (depending on size), peeled and thickly sliced

500 g/1 lb 2 oz unrefined cane sugar

1 finger's length vanilla pod, split to expose the seeds

about 500 ml/18 fl oz water

300 ml/10 fl oz whipping cream or canned condensed milk

The guava, a native of Ecuador and Peru, is usually about the size of a large pear (although variable), with a subtle flowery fragrance and soft, slightly grainy flesh that varies in colour from a deep rose to creamy white.

Put the guavas and bananas in a small heavy-based saucepan with the sugar, vanilla pod and water – just enough to cover the fruit. Bring to the boil, then reduce the heat, cover loosely and cook gently for 30–40 minutes, or until the fruit is a rich dark red and the juices thicken to a clear syrup.

Remove from the heat and leave to cool. Remove the vanilla pod and scrape the seeds into the juices. Transfer the fruit and syrup to a blender or food processor and blend to a purée.

Whip the cream until thick enough to hold soft peaks, and fold into the fruit purée. Transfer to a serving dish, cover and chill in the refrigerator for at least 2 hours before serving. Alternatively, transfer to a lidded plastic freezerproof container, freeze for 2–3 hours, or until firm, and serve as a parfait.

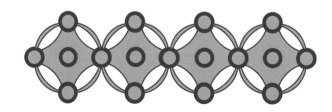

# Chocolate pecan brownies with chilli

*Biscochitos de chocolate y nueces con chilli*

**Makes 12**

50 g/1³/4 oz unsalted butter, softened, plus extra for greasing

100 g/3¹/2 oz unrefined cane sugar

3 eggs, beaten

100 g/3¹/2 oz self-raising flour

75 g/2³/4 oz cocoa powder

1 tsp dried chilli flakes

about 1 tbsp rum

100 g/3¹/2 oz pecan nut halves

Gorgeously sticky, chewy brownies with a difference – a chilli flavouring subtle enough to wake up the taste buds without shocking the palate. The Aztecs and Mayans considered their chilli-flavoured drinking chocolate the food of the gods.

Preheat the oven to 180°C/350°F/Gas Mark 4. Grease a 20-cm/8-inch square or equivalent-sized rectangular shallow baking tin or tray.

Using a wooden spoon, beat the butter with sugar in a warmed bowl until pale and fluffy. Alternatively, process in a food processor. Beat in the eggs, a little at a time, adding a little flour if the mixture begins to curdle. Switching to a metal spoon, gently fold in the flour, cocoa powder and chilli flakes. Stir in the rum and add enough water until you have a cake mixture that drops easily from the spoon. Taste and see if you need to add a little more chilli. Fold in the pecan nuts, reserving a few of the best for the top.

Pour the cake mixture into the prepared tin, smoothing it into the corners. Sprinkle the top with the reserved pecan nuts.

Bake in the preheated oven for 20–25 minutes, or until crusted on top but still not quite set. Remove from the oven and cut into 12 squares while still warm. Transfer to a wire rack to cool and set.

# Index